Throwing Rocks

To Danielle
Be immovable!
Be courageous!
Lindsey Acton

Written by

Lindsey Acton

Edited and published by

Tom Brew

Hilltop30 Publishing Group, LLC

THROWING ROCKS

©2020 by Hilltop30 Publishing Group, LLC

ISBN Number: 978-1-949616-13-2

Library of Congress Control Number: Pending

This is a work of nonfiction.

To contact author Lindsey Acton:
Website: www.lindseyactonstories.com
Email: lindseyactonstories@gmail.com

To contact Hilltop30 Publishing Group, LLC:
Website: www.hilltop30.com
Email: tombrew@hilltop30.com
Phone: (727) 412-4008

For multiple copies of this book or to arrange book signings and/or speaking engagements, please feel free to email or call Tom Brew at Hilltop30 Publishing Group, LLC.

Printed in the United States of America.

<u>DEDICATION</u>

*For Trish, who gave me
the homework assignment
that saved my life.*

PUBLISHER'S NOTE

During my four decades as a reporter and editor at some of America's finest newspapers, it's always been important to me to tell stories that matter. That's been my first rule — along with always doing it right — and it's been no different during the five years that I've owned my media publishing company.

Lindsey Acton has a story that matters. A lot. And I'm excited to publish it and share it with the world.

I've written, edited or published nearly two dozen books now, and many of them have dealt with mental health issues in some way, shape or form. It's a topic that's very important to me, and has been for most of my life.

This one is important, too, and it's a beautifully told story that is both deep and emotional. During the past year that we've worked on this book, we've both shed a few tears along the way.

At the end of this project, Lindsey and I had a big decision to make. Because an important part of this story deals with teenagers in a high school setting, we went back and forth about whether we should use their real names, and her school location. The journalist in me thought we should. It's just how I've always told stories.

Because this is Lindsey's story and all that she's been through, she didn't want the re-telling of it to hurt anyone, so we agreed to change names, of the people and the school. Because I had one last concern, I wanted to take a moment before you read this story to make one thing perfectly clear.

Everything you read in this story is 100 percent true. It

all happened. And I don't want you to think that just because we changed names that we changed facts or emphasis. We did not. There is nothing fictional, nothing embellished. This is a true story of a young teacher and the trauma she endured, and lives with to this day.

So please absorb every word of this, and let it sink in. I share stories like this because I want to help the next person who is even remotely close to a situation like this, be it a teacher, a student, a friend or a parent.

A story that matters? Absolutely.

Lindsey has written a tremendous book here. It's a great story, and it will make a difference. I'm sure you will feel her emotion, too, through every page. Thank you for reading — and sharing her story with others.

Tom Brew
President & Editor
Hilltop30 Publishing Group, LLC

Chapter

Becoming the Teacher

My alarm was set for 5 a.m., but it didn't really matter. I had been up most of the night anyway, tossing and turning and burning off nervous energy, wondering why the numbers on my clock were moving so slowly. I slept some, but I know it wasn't much.

When you're a teacher on the night before the first day of school, that's just the way it is.

There are multipliers for that anxiety when it's your first-ever first day as a teacher, and as a 23-year-old in a small suburban town in central Indiana in August of 2006, I was a bit of a disaster in those early-morning hours. My fears and concerns were significant. When it was finally time to move, I sat up in bed, swung my legs over the edge, and headed to the shower, ready to attempt to make myself seem like an adult professional. That wasn't going to be easy. I was supposed to be totally prepared for this after hanging an education degree on my wall, but as I showered, I couldn't help but think that these kids – many of whom were only four years younger than I was – would have absolutely no interest in listening to a word I had to say.

As I shampooed my hair, so many negative thoughts danced around in my head. How would I introduce myself?

How would I get them to listen long enough to set up a seating chart? How would I best relay the expectations for my classroom? Even more scary, how would I uphold those expectations? How would I ever convince them that I had even a remote idea of what I was doing, especially when I seriously doubted that fact myself?

Those thoughts lingered as I finished getting ready that morning – and in some ways, I've learned, they linger forever in some form. Even fourteen years later, I know they never truly leave you when you're a teacher, they just freak you out at varying levels through the years as you learn to trust yourself more.

So here I was, sleep-deprived, anxious, and doing my level best to look unafraid. I was living with my mom in that small town, and she insisted on taking a "first day of school" picture, just like we did every year when I was the student. I told her I was the teacher now, and that this tradition would no longer be necessary, but she would have nothing of it. To her, the first day of school is the first day, no matter which side of the desk I was going to sit on.

"You're still going to school on the first day, so the rule is, I get a picture," she said to me with a smile. This is one of her traditions that I love and appreciate, though there were plenty of years when I protested. We took the picture, and she was happy. Even now, fourteen years later, I still make sure she gets a first-day picture, though these days a husband, a couple kids and a dog have been added to that mix.

I remember choosing carefully what I was going to wear that day, going for something professional, yet stylish.

I put on a cardigan and capri pants with heels, thinking surely this would send the message that I was a serious professional. I even fixed my hair – maybe if I took some extra time, I thought, I would look a little older and maybe I would even fit the part. It was a huge fear that morning that I was going to look younger than my own students. And that fear was real.

Outside of being nauseous and nervous. arriving to school wasn't a problem because I had made that short little six-minute drive from my mom's house to the high school hundreds of times as a student. But this time was different. I never thought this would happen since I had vowed to never teach at my old high school.

Yet, here I was, so well-prepared to start my teaching career in classrooms that I had grown up in myself. When I was a student here, I wanted to be a teacher.

Now, I was the teacher.

I thought I knew everything I needed to know. I could teach these kids English, and share my love of books and stories with them. Bring it on. In college, we were warned that our first year in a classroom would be the toughest year of our lives, but I just brushed that off. Surely they were exaggerating, I thought.

They weren't.

In reality, I had absolutely no idea what I was getting into. To say that I was totally unprepared for the drama and intensity that swirls through a high school classroom is a massive understatement.

I was clueless.

And, as a fresh-faced 23-year-old, I had no chance.

*** *** ***

How did I get to my old high school when the thought of teaching there was always −NEVER!!? Well, the story starts with ice cream.

The career path for me, even from a young age, was going to be teaching. But after I graduated from college in December of 2005, I was having some doubts and decided to take a job that summer as a behavior consultant with a firm that provided residential services for adults with various developmental disabilities. I traveled from group home to group home, gathering data on the adults and their behavioral patterns. When I finished, I would return to the office and examine the data in conjunction with their medication information to determine why a resident might have changed in the way he or she acted. I would then make a speculation as to whether a type of medication change could have contributed to this altered behavior.

In truth, it was a pretty boring job, but since I was doubting my decision to teach, it was a job that served me well.

At least for a while.

In a matter of months after accepting the position, they changed the type of work I was doing. The hours became longer, more intense, and less about where my passion lied – with people. I have always needed people and human interaction, even though I profess to be a closet introvert. While I need solitude, I thrive on human interaction, and this job was rapidly removing those connections from my life. I started to miss teaching, and interacting with both teenagers and adults.

I was having a bad day at work, so I stopped at a local ice cream and fast food place for lunch. As I was waiting for my food, I heard a familiar, "Lindsey?" As I whirled around to see which small-town citizen recognized me, I saw it was my own high school English teacher, Elaine Carey. We had a long conversation, but the basic summation of it was this: they needed an English teacher, and did I, by any chance at all, need a job?

As a matter of fact, I did.

I answered her: "I actually think I do. What did you have in mind?"

We spent the next hour talking about what the job would entail, what I would be teaching, and how it would be set up. I grew more excited about the possibility by the minute. Was this really happening? Maybe I was supposed to be a teacher after all – maybe my "break" from education was over in a matter of six months or so, and maybe, just maybe, I would have a classroom of my own sooner rather than later.

Just a few hours later, Elaine called and asked if I would be available for an interview the following day. Of course, I said that I was. The interview was fairly painless – though it was very intimidating to sit in front of a room full of people who had been partially responsible for my ability to be there in the first place. Our Guidance Director, Jenny French, was my counselor when I was in high school. Elaine had been my Honors English teacher for two years, and Shonda Haver had been my speech teacher. The only person in the room who had not directly contributed to my own education was Jane Berensen, the principal who was fairly new to our little community. They offered me the job a few days later, and I said yes. What a week. I had inquired about, interviewed for, and been offered a position teaching high school English in the one place I declared I never wanted to work: my own former high school.

I guess "never say never" is a real phrase. "Never" is one of those words that we throw around, that we use casually to express our aversion to a task or scenario in our lives. Right then, though, I learned that a person's checklist of "nevers" quickly can be replaced. Life truly can be one way one day, and it can be a completely different way the very next day.

Just like that, I was right back at my old school.

That seemed surreal to me. I had moved to my hometown when I was eleven years old, and I made a ton of great friends. My mom was there, my younger siblings were there. My own little brother was going to be a freshman in the very school I was teaching at.

Those were all reasons for NOT wanting to teach there in the first place. I had wanted something else. For a long time, I wanted to work in a place completely different from this one. A place with more people – more kinds of people – and not just ones who looked like me. I thought I wanted to live elsewhere, that the small town life just was not for me. I wasn't sure I was prepared to live and work in the community where I had mostly grown up. I didn't know how in the world I would work with people who had been my own teachers. How was I ever going to call them by their first names? How could my favorite math teacher, Miss Stemp, suddenly become just Laura to me?

We had one grocery store in my town. Did I really want to be stopped by parents in the aisles to discuss their students' grades? No, I really didn't. And so, I said "never," tempted fate, and found out exactly what happens when a person makes a declaration based on her own plans rather than those already laid out by the forces of the universe.

Just like that, I went from "never" wanting to be there to being so happy to walk through those doors once again.

*** *** ***

When I slid my key into my classroom door, I felt that shadow of doubt creep back in. It hit me, and hit me hard. What if I mess this up? What if I do it all wrong today and the whole year – my whole teaching career – is ruined? What if I made a mistake leaving a good job for something I wasn't even sure I really wanted to do?

Something told me to keep going, so I turned the key, pushed open the door, and hauled in all my "necessities" – books, pens, calendars, snacks, Diet Coke. You name it, it was in the bag.

As I started to arrange my things, I gazed out across the rows of empty desks. There is nothing like the quiet in a school before the students arrive. It's almost eerie, as if the life of the building has been sucked out, only to be breathed back in by bells, by student laughter, and by their daily shuffling about. The quietness of the room stopped me in my tracks for a moment as I sat down at my desk for the first time ever. In that moment, I finally felt like this room was mine, that these classes were mine, and that these students – whoever they were – belonged to me, and me to them.

As I surveyed my room, I imagined it coming to life

with the movements and the voices of the students who would be walking through that door within the hour. I imagined those young people sitting in those desks, considering my request to please take me seriously, and I remembered not long ago being the one on the other side, the one sizing up the teacher.

It hadn't been too terribly long ago that I was right where they would be – acting and feeling like they did. From the big desk, the world looked so different. How was I ever going to do this the way I wanted to do it? How was I ever going to explain to them how much it meant to me to be up there, talking about books and reading with them? From the big desk, mistakes could be more significant and they meant more – actual human lives were my responsibility for these seven hours of each day. And even though I felt ready, I simultaneously felt a terror that came from a place that was so deep and so new, that I couldn't identify the origin. Moments later, the bell rang, and as my students filed in, I took a deep breath and stood up, feeling my legs tremble in those high heels as I greeted my first group of students.

In that moment, I became the teacher.

The first day was fairly easy. I knew what to expect, the kids were relatively well-behaved, and it ended largely without incident. For a job that I wasn't really sure I wanted, this one started out well. I went home that evening as tired as I have ever been in my life, and I stayed at least that tired for the next ten months.

On that day, though, I was focused on the now and, at least for the moment, I was able to stop and reflect, if only briefly, on the events that brought me to this place, and the rapidity with which they had occurred.

*** *** ***

I am always comfortable at my mom's house, so living with her at age 23 wasn't unusual. I had grown up, yes, but I still liked that feeling of being "home" with her. I had recently made my very first "adult" purchase – a dog. As I look back now, I think about it and laugh at how, at that time, my personal measure of adulthood was owning a dog. It seemed like such a grown-up, sophisticated thing to do, so Lily the Boston Terrier came to live with me at my mom's house.

My routine changed immediately. I went from setting my own hours on the old job to being back on "school time." I found myself at work before 6:30 a.m. most days, planning and preparing, and on the days I wasn't working on lessons, I was running or swimming before school. Getting in a good sweat three days a week or so has always been essential for me to remain sane and steady, and because I was so exhausted by the end of my work day, working out in the morning was about the only way to get it in. Most evenings, I was at school until after 4 p.m., preparing for my next day. Many times at night, I would grade papers at home until well after dark.

It was exhausting, and there was never an end in sight.

As I settled into teaching these juniors and seniors, the battles with kids who were only four or five or six years younger than me had begun. It was beyond difficult to assert authority over these teens, because they looked at me and thought they saw a friend or a peer, but then were met with resistance and firm authority from me. Every day brought its own issues – excessive talking from one student, inappropriate comments from another, backtalk or sass from someone else.

Teacher school prepares young professionals for these hypothetical classrooms full of students wanting to learn. I was taught that. I am also sure we had our fair share of discussions about discipline, but I don't really know that we spent a bunch of time learning teaching methods for the thirty different personalities we encounter during any given class period. I was taught how to talk to them, and talk with them, but I was never taught how to figure out what they were thinking, or why they acted the way they did.

I also don't think there was a class for what to do when you, as the teacher, don't LOOK any older than the students you're teaching.

There was no class to prepare me for the junior boys trying to impress their 23-year-old teacher who probably still looked like a teenager herself. There was no class to remind me, also, that the only way a junior boy knows how to try to impress anyone is by being as obnoxious as possible and seeing how many of his friends would laugh. Apparently, this is the measuring stick of success at that age, and because I never was a teenage boy, I either did not know, or I forgot that this would be something I could face early in my career.

I really didn't know what to do. In one group, the boys were on the football team, so after several days of practically begging them to hush so I could teach, I finally contacted their coach. I've learned there is no faster way to inspire students to straighten up than to show them that all of their teachers and coaches talk to each other all of the time.

And in a small community, this was a universal truth whose value I totally underestimated. Just a few emails back and forth with the head coach and a couple episodes of running as punishment, and those boys started being model citizens in my English class, and my worries with them were over. Fourteen years into my career, it's now extremely rare that I have to contact ANYONE for help with a student, but at the time, I sure appreciated the help. At 23. my relative lack of preparation for the unique nature of student personalities made for a challenging set of circum-stances.

None of that had anything to do with the content I was supposed to be teaching them. I fought battles like these almost daily, and my energy and enthusiasm for my job began to wane. These battles allowed me to quickly realize how naive I really was. I had no idea what I was doing. I found myself exhausted, both physically and emotionally, with absolutely no coping skills to make any of it different or better.

There's truth to the difficulty and soul-sucking nature of a first year of teaching that cannot be learned without first personally experiencing it. That first day – and every day for a year – I learned the true definition of exhaustion. At age 23, as I stood in front of these teenagers, I had no idea that I was about to begin what I still believe in my heart – even after facing significant, heartbreaking struggles – to be the single-most difficult year of my life.

That first day, it was just a start. It was hard, and it would only get harder.

Much harder.

Chapter

How Columbine Changed Everything

I **never considered** school violence when I made the decision to become a teacher. I never even thought about mental health – my own or anyone else's – when I was in high school. And I definitely never considered that a school – the place in the world where, for my entire life, I felt the most capable and the most comfortable – could ever be a place wrought with violence, fear, and uncertainty.

Why would I have? School had always come easy for me. I was a great student, and I felt safe in a school. There would have been no reason for me, in my quest for a career in education, to ever think that a place where I felt so comfortable could ever be associated with violence. And there certainly was no reason why I would ever have thought that the person or people engaging in these violent acts would be one of their own – a child.

The first time I had to wrap my head around a violent incident occurring in a school, I was a 16-year-old high school sophomore. It was April of 1999, and Dylan Klebold and Eric Harris had just opened fire inside Columbine High School in Colorado, mowing down 13 of their classmates before taking their own lives. On that day, for the first time in my life, I watched the entire United States collectively suck in and hold its breath while coverage of this heinous crime dominated the news. As a young journalism student who spent most of her free time around and with other young high school journalists, I vividly remember spending hours after school in my journalism teacher's classroom with the TV on, marveling at the horror that was unfolding in front of us.

In the 1990s, acts of mass violence like Columbine were significantly less common than they are now and, as a result, our shock and distress over the incident stayed with me for years. What impacted me perhaps more than the event itself was our teacher and how she handled it around us. At the time, I had just discovered high school journalism, and felt very strongly that I wanted to be a reporter. The excitement of covering the news and my passion for writing seemed to merge at just the perfect place, laying out for me what I thought at the time was an obvious career path.

But our teacher, Christine Campbell, used Columbine as the perfect teachable moment. We covered the event, talked about it, processed our feelings, and really worked through how this tragedy could have ever happened in the first place. Her kindness and compassion through this event – and through so many others years – demonstrated to me what adults were supposed to do and be in circumstances like these. She showed us that out of tragedy can come some beautiful lessons – and some shockingly beautiful demon-strations of human compassion, both at home and around the world.

The rest of my high school days were spent pursuing

my journalistic passion. I worked hard on improving my writing, figuring out how I could make a career out of writing the news, and then ultimately deciding that what had been more impactful for me was who I did that work with, not the work itself.

There is no replacement in one's life for an effective teacher – for one who takes the time to talk, to listen, and to understand. I had this in Campbell – that's what we called her, and she didn't mind – and I thought this meant that all teachers were like her. If ever they weren't, I thought they should be. She became the standard by which I measured all other educators, myself included, for the rest of my life.

It was her influence that led me to make a different career choice by the time I was ready to apply to college. Instead of journalism, I was going to study to become a high school English teacher. Although Campbell is no longer working in education – she's now a missionary in South America – her gentle nature, her kind words, and her ability to challenge my thinking with just the right question are traits I always hope my students would say I possess in my own approach to teaching.

While I always felt most comfortable in a school building, I didn't always consider that I would want to spend the rest of my life in one. In my years growing up, when my only true passions were reading and writing, my dad would tell me that the way to figure out what I wanted to be when I grew up was to find something I loved and then find a way to get paid to do it.

Looking back, this was probably some of the best advice I ever received from him or anyone else, but I still didn't think, as a sophomore in high school, that teaching was my path. Sure, I was an excellent student – I got good grades, and because I was a passionate writer and a people pleaser, my teachers (mostly) appreciated my approach to school. And I appreciated theirs. I was hungry for the knowledge they were imparting, and I wanted to learn what they had to teach. Those relationships worked well. I loved being at school.

Looking back, teaching was such an obvious path for me because I still think our society needs people who are passionate about writing and about learning. And yes, we even need people who are passionate about and willing to work with teenagers. One of the best parts about what I do is the conversations I have every day and the relationships I build. Learning about my students and where they come from is a sacred privilege, and I owe my teaching style and my ability to convince reluctant kids to comply and even to do good work once in a while to Campbell, and to the skills I learned from her.

So, when I stood in front of my own classroom as a 23-year-old not even ten years after the tragedy at Columbine High School, nowhere near the forefront of my mind was there any thought about mental health or the complexities of these young people in front of me. The only thing I could think about in that moment was the full-circle nature of the path my life had taken. Here I was teaching, in my own classroom, just three doors down from where I received the most influential teaching of my own life.

Little did I know I would draw from Campbell's wisdom and strength multiple times throughout that first school year, that her gentle nature would guide me through some of my darkest days, and that her handling of my classmates – and of me – when we were just teens ourselves would ultimately be the reason I didn't walk out of my classroom at the end of that first year and never go back.

I could have walked out. Easily.

But I didn't.

Chapter

Survival

While I expected that my first year of teaching would be difficult, I totally underestimated the level of hardship I would face. I knew that grading and planning and learning a new curriculum would be hard – really hard. But never once did I consider, even for a second, that I also was still a human being, and that I had a family and friends and a personal life and a world that still turned, even as I tried to navigate the demands of my new life. Before long, I settled into a steady routine of 12-hour days – on a good day – and evenings spent with a red pen, grading away.

Before the days of the balanced calendar that most schools use now, we started school in mid-August. This left about two solid weeks of school before we took a small breather for a three-day Labor Day weekend. Right about this time, I remember feeling like perhaps I was starting to hit my stride – maybe I was settling in just a little bit. Did I have more free time or was I less tired? No. I was just growing accustomed to my eyes feeling like sandpaper and my teacher bag feeling extremely full.

A few weeks after school started, we had our Open House,

or Back to School Night, in which our students' parents could come in and meet their child's teacher. I know it doesn't seem like a significant day, but for the rest of my life, I will remember my very first Back to School Night because it was the night everything changed in my world. My year became even harder in ways I could never have predicted. Things came at me from all angles, and set the stage for challenges that I could not even have considered at that time.

For as long as I can remember, I have been a Mama's Girl. My mom is my person – and has been my entire life. I am blessed to have two great parents, but there's just always been something different and significant about my relationship with my mom. We talk daily, even now. Rarely did I then – or do I now – make major decisions without her. We've always been connected in a way that I never understood until I had my own son in 2015. In my first year of teaching, I hadn't left the safety of her home yet, and she still epitomized security for me in every possible way. She was 44 years old when I started teaching – I had never even considered her youth because it was all I ever knew – but on that warm August day, her youth was ALL I could consider as my world narrowed, my vision tunneled, and the only reaction I was able to muster in was to literally beg the universe for mercy.

That day? You guessed it. Open House Day.

I had just enough time to go home for dinner between the end of my school day and the parents' arrival later that evening. When I got home, my mom was sitting on the couch, and she asked me to sit down. I don't remember all of this conversation, but the summation of it was that she had been to the doctor, and the doctor had some concerns. She had some tests run, my mom said, and they were awaiting the results. The final tidbit she gave me before the world went silent was that I should probably expect an official cancer diagnosis within the week.

Cancer?

What?

How could she have cancer when she was only 44 years old? What kind of cancer? How did they find it? How were they planning to get it OUT of her body?

I found myself reeling, unable to say much. I've learned, several years and several therapy sessions later, that silence is a coping mechanism of mine. Is it the healthiest way to handle my struggles? Probably not, but it's what I do. I have a tendency to stop talking, to go dark, when I have to face a problem or a situation that feels bigger than what I think I can handle. Indeed, my mom was right: the next week, she was diagnosed with Stage 3C ovarian cancer. I didn't know it at the time, but this diagnosis would be the scene-setter for the rest of that school year.

Just as quickly as I had changed jobs and started my new life, our family was turned on its head. Suddenly, we were dealing with a late-stage cancer diagnosis that yields a five-year survival rate of only about 25 percent. Hearing these statistics, coupled with the treatment plan that would ultimately save my mom's life, was surreal.

This surely wasn't happening. Not in our family, not with my mom.

And yet, no matter how hard I tried to go silent, to stay silent, and to be in perfect denial that the very real possibility of losing the most important person in my life was smacking me in the face, I could not escape it. I could not run.

I wanted to – boy, did I want to. But life has a funny way of coming back around and reminding a person that she must stand up and face her challenges.

*** *** ***

Maybe that was the real lesson from my first year. Maybe it's what I was supposed to learn, peripherally, even if it was clothed in trauma and heartbreak. Maybe, all these years later, I am supposed to have learned how to not hide or struggle or go dark when I should be asking for help. I like to think we learn our lessons – even if we learn them the hard way – through these types of experiences so we can pass along our wisdom to others in their times of need. The eternal teacher in me needs to believe this, needs to trust that this is part of the process. Otherwise, how does a person cope in a world with so much sadness?

Remembering myself as a human being was not something I did well that year. Instead, I threw myself into my job, working even more hours. None of that made the challenges at home go away, and none of that made being a first-year teacher any easier – but I had to try. So into my work I dove, channeling my stress the best I could. Because I'm a person who needs physical activity, I started there. Using the pool a few mornings a week for a vigorous swim made for a relaxing, refreshing start to my day, and I easily fell into this comfortable routine.

It was comfortable until one morning when I received a phone call at my desk.

The basic issue was this: A father was absolutely incensed that I had the audacity to use the school's pool in the morning. As a member of the teaching staff, he said, I should worry more about distracting young boys by walking around the pool deck wearing a swimsuit than I should about my own need or desire for physical fitness. Didn't I understand how I was tempting them? Didn't I understand that it was inappropriate for a teacher to be in a swimsuit anywhere near a teenage boy?

Yes, I know. Of course, I know. I was a swimmer in high school, and a Division I swimmer in college at IUPUI in Indianapolis. Those mornings where I would swim at my high school, I wasn't in a skimpy bikini; I was in a swimsuit that I would have raced in and, trust me, those suits are not built for fashion.

The ridiculousness of this phone call was exacerbated by the fact that this parent hammered his point home for more than 45 minutes, and in that time he did not care to hear – not even once – that as a member of the community, I had a right to use the pool if I wanted to. No, instead, my saying a quick hello to his son that morning as I went into the locker room to shower had made him "uncomfortable," and he demanded that I cease using the pool immediately.

In another life, I wish I could go back and react to this father again. I wish I could tell him how absolutely ridiculous his request was, how incredibly presumptuous it was of him to suggest that I had anything to do with his son's discomfort – if it did in fact exist – or that somehow my exercise had anything to do with him or with his son in the first place.

But it wasn't another life, and at that time, at that age, I didn't know what else to do. So, I stopped using the pool. Looking back, I understand the decision. I understand that it was rooted in fear. But I am still frustrated by the bullying from that parent and how I responded to it, because I didn't know any better. Because I didn't have a support system to ask about issues like this – because when in my wildest imagination would I have thought something like this would have ever come up? Today, I would have no problem explaining myself to a parent like this, but I'm also 37; I'm someone's mother – and frankly, these interactions have stopped in this somewhat "seasoned" phase of my teaching career.

*** *** ***

As it turned out, bullying was a theme that first year – one that I was not expecting from parents, certainly, but also one that I was not expecting from my own colleagues, either. As it turns out, looking no older than one's students does a teacher no favors. It also apparently reflects poorly with female colleagues who just aren't sure how to react to a brand new, enthusiastic teacher. That's how I viewed myself at the time. I never considered my appearance to be prohibitive in any way, or that it would compromise me professionally. And I certainly never considered that middle-aged women could be so catty and immature. But I quickly found out some of them were.

In my first few weeks as a teacher, I was assigned, as all first-year teachers are, a mentor teacher to walk me through the year, answering questions and providing support. My mentor just happened to be a man. A single man named Matt.

Cue the mania from the middle-aged women.

One colleague in particular really struggled with this, even going so far as to demand that I be fired for "flirting" with my mentor. We could not even laugh together or tell jokes without being the subject of her scrutiny. This went on for years, but it was the worst in that first year. These women I worked with absolutely could not handle my partnership with this colleague – or the fact that he and I had hit it off and became fast friends.

We talked often, and as my first year was shaping up to be such a difficult one, he was aware of it all and was a support system for me the duration of my mom's cancer journey. I leaned heavily on him at different times. For many years, he was my "work husband," but there was nothing beyond a friendship. Not ever.

I went to his wedding. I befriended his wife. I helped him name his dogs. I recommended books and TV shows to him, and he did the same for me. I owe my *Game of Thrones* obsession solely to him. Our relationship was always pla-tonic, but in 2006, not a single middle-aged female teacher wanted to hear or believe that our friendship was simply that between a male and a female, and carried no romantic undertones.

More than a decade later, I understand now that this colleague who insisted I be fired was in some serious pain herself. She was in a horrible marriage to an abusive alcoholic, and not too long into the school year, she started divorce proceedings and moved back in with her parents until she could get on her feet. I don't know if she knows I was aware of what was happening behind the scenes, both with her divorce and with her insistence that my relationship with Matt was inappropriate, but I do know – now – that people who are in pain themselves tend to inflict pain on others, whether it be intentional or otherwise. It took a long time for me to find peace with the fact that her reactions likely had nothing at all to do with me – that her reactions to me came from a place of her own pain, and that the only way she knew to cope with these painful parts of her life was to hurt others. Armed with very few of her own healthy coping mechanisms, she instead turned on me, using her "hatred" for me as an outlet for her pain.

During this time, I remember asking Matt, so many times, if I could just march into her classroom and confront her. He never did advise me to do that, but instead he suggested I just prove her wrong. In my immaturity, I would ask him why I always had to be the bigger person: "Why do I have to eat a shit sandwich with a smile on my face while she is spending all of her spare time torturing me?"

He would remind me that part of being a professional is not always being allowed to, or able to, say what is on one's mind, but that messages can be communicated clearly – sometimes even more clearly than through words – by our actions and our reactions. And so, I did no confronting that year. In fact, I never confronted her. I continued to be kind and respectful, but I also kept my distance as much as I could to avoid giving her further fodder for discussion.

It largely didn't help, because her distaste for me spanned a number of years. I do think in the decade that has followed that she and I have reached a place of peace. I would even say that she is a friend. We have talked, laughed, cried and hugged – so even if at the time my inability to confront her really bothered me, Matt was right. It paid off in the end because I've gained a person who respects me, and who I also respect. That's much more valuable than any confrontation I could have orchestrated in my mind that first year.

It seemed like planning and teaching English became such a small part of my day. Instead, I was answering for my youthful appearance at every level; I was watching my mom fight, clawing tooth-and-nail, to stay alive long enough to see my brother graduate from high school, and I was doing my best to build relationships with these students whose educations partially rested on my shoulders – all the while attempting to stay at least ONE day ahead of them in my planning.

As you can imagine, I really could have used a life raft about four weeks into my first year of teaching, because I absolutely felt like I was drowning.

*** *** ***

On one particularly difficult day where I had found myself practically gasping for air, I met Kevin for the first time. Sure, he'd been sitting in the same desk in my fifth-period class for the last month, but until this day, he had never spoken to me. I can remember back to when I stood in front of my class, teaching, that he would watch me intently, seemingly listening to every word I said. I had been given no reason to get on him for his behavior, and I also hadn't had much time or opportunity to establish many other relationships with kids, especially ones that were based on positivity. So, when I found myself at my desk, head in my hands, wondering how I was ever going to survive – cancer, teaching, and bullies were really taking their toll on this particular day – it took me somewhat by surprise to hear an unfamiliar voice.

"You hanging in there?"

I looked up to find the voice in the nearly-empty classroom. It was Kevin.

Somewhat surprised, I answered, "Sort of. Sorry. I'm fine. What's up?"

"You just seem like you're having a tough day. And you look REALLY tired," he said.

I laughed. I remember the laugh vividly. And then I said, "Yeah, tired is a word for it."

"Well, don't let them get you down. You're doing a good job. They're all a bunch of assholes."

I wanted to start in on his language, but instead of correcting him, I said, "Thank you. It's just been a tough week."

He chuckled – a chuckle I would hear many more times in the coming months – and then turned to leave my room. As he walked away, he said, "Try to ignore them."

For the first time in what felt like forever, a human interaction made me smile instead of making me feel angry, or making me cry. It felt like a hand from the universe, extended to remind me that I was there for those kids, not for any of the peripheral nonsense that had consumed most of my first several weeks as a teacher.

Accepting advice from a teenager wasn't something I was used to, but at the time, I was taking any smile I could get.

I had no idea how temporary that smile was.

Chapter

Kevin

When I went home to teach, all I knew was that this small central Indiana town was my safe place. We moved around so much when I was a little kid that staying here for a considerable length of time was a really big deal. I wasn't born there, but it had become my home. And the only place I felt more secure than in that town itself was at my mom's house. Living there felt normal, natural. As a new teacher with a car payment and some student loans, I couldn't afford to live on my own. Since I spent the majority of my childhood, adolescence, and young-adult life there, why wouldn't it feel like the safest place in the world for me?

Even when life events took me away from home, my connection to my mom and to my hometown always brought me back to the place where I felt the most connected. I was sustained by the stability of my home, so home I went, and being there was a blessing. My mom's cancer diagnosis drew our family together, and I needed to be with my parents and my siblings.

They needed me, and I needed them. No one was handling it well, and I was, perhaps, handling it the worst of everyone. Regardless of my initial feelings about taking a job in this town, there was something so warm and inviting about being home, so I allowed those feelings of safety to envelop me and to overshadow the doubts I initially had about being back at my alma mater.

My coping mechanisms, while not always healthy even to this day, essentially include becoming a turtle. These characteristics include pulling inside my shell, going silent, and avoiding pain as much as I can. In the time since the events of that first year took place, I have worked diligently on how I cope with stress, and though I'm better than I used to be at handling it, I still have some turtle tendencies that take me by surprise now and then when situations in life become too overwhelming or too difficult.

After my mom's cancer diagnosis, I became even more like a turtle: I pulled in more than I ever had before. Now my home life included chemotherapy, wigs, repeated blood tests, and massive surgeries for my mom. I was absolutely unable to cope with what was happening to her, and fear overtook me. It shook me to my core, and it demanded a response. But the only response I could execute was to pull in, to go dark, and to avoid.

I was incapable of facing what was happening around me because the person who had been my safety, who was my home, was facing death.

At age 23, all I could think about was what she would miss: I was still single, but I would still think about her never meeting her grandkids. My brother was only 14 years old, and she would miss so much of his life, too. My brain filled with these negative possibilities, and no matter how hard I tried, I could not push them out of my mind. They consumed me, striking within me a fear that I had never felt before, and that I was unable to harness or to understand.

As I write this story now, my mom is eleven years free of cancer. She has hugged and rocked and loved all of her grandbabies, and she absolutely cheered with pride when my brother accepted his high school diploma four years after her initial diagnosis. She zipped up my wedding dress, and on that day, she carried my flowers for me while I carried my skirt. She helped me fold baby clothes as I prepared for my son's arrival – all things I feared she would never get to do. At the time of her diagnosis and subsequent treatment, I had no ability to see the other side – or even to trust that there was one.

Instead of celebrating the early positive news that surgery and treatment were working, I mourned a loss. Cancer, you see, never really leaves you once it's come and gone. A person's body may be free of cancer, but contemplating the mortality of my primary parent – the stability in my life, the one who kept it all together when it should have all fallen apart, the one who not only believed in, but who was responsible for, every little thing about the person I was from the day I was born – never really left me. Those worries were more than I could handle at that stage of my life.

Like the turtle, I created a shell of protection. The predators I was hiding from were cancer and death, and the only way I knew to protect myself was to draw in – head, limbs, everything, and only expose myself to danger if it was absolutely necessary.

*** *** ***

Rarely was my head out of my shell that year, much less very far above water, so when Kevin found me in my classroom that day with my head in my hands and offered what appeared to be a friendly face, not only did it make me smile, but it felt normal. It felt like my first interaction in weeks that wasn't with something that scared or threatened me. I didn't feel the need to draw in or to protect myself.

For several weeks, my conversations with Kevin continued somewhat casually. A "hello" here or a "how's it going" there was the basic extent of it. He would smile when he came into class instead of just walking to his desk and not engaging at all, as he had done previously. Until this point, he had been rather inconspicuous – not much participation, but definitely no discipline problems. He would watch me teach, appearing to listen. I do remember a couple times now where I felt like he was staring intently at me, because I found the intensity of his concentration to be somewhat unnerving.

At the time, I couldn't have articulated what, if anything, bothered me about what I was watching from the other side of the big desk. I just kept teaching, and smiling back when he smiled at me. He gave me absolutely no reason to feel like I couldn't – or shouldn't – have that kind of interaction with him.

The first time I had a long-ish conversation with Kevin was after class one day. He hung around after the bell, looking around the room, and I could tell he was hesitant, but that he had something he really needed to say.

"Hey! What's up?" I asked him.

"Nada. Just chillin'. How are you?"

"I'm fine, thanks. Still pretty tired," I said with a smile.

He returned the smile, "I bet so. Hey, listen. I heard you had some trouble with Ethan a couple weeks ago."

"Ethan?" I didn't immediately know what he was talking about.

"Yeah, at the pool?" he answered.

"Oh, that," I said. The unpleasant memory flooded my mind as I tried to push it away, to not think about the absolutely awful interaction I had with Ethan's dad, and to forget this negative thing had ever even happened.

"Yeah, I heard him talking about you in choir. It wasn't cool," Kevin said.

"What do you mean?" I asked.

"Well, he may or may not have made some comments about what it might have been like to see his teacher in a swimsuit."

I remember rolling my eyes. I also remember my cheeks flushing and struggling to keep the conversation moving. What was his end game here? Why did he know about this? And more importantly, why was he bringing it up now?

I responded, "Oh, Lord."

"Yeah," Kevin said, "Apparently he was a fan."

I was incredulous,

"What? He told his dad he was uncomfortable around me," I blurted out before I could stop myself.

Kevin laughed again – that same chuckle from the last time we had talked after class: "I don't think the type of uncomfortable he was … is the type of uncomfortable you're thinking of."

Mortified, feeling my face flush, I said, "Well, it's over

now. I'm not worried about it."

Kevin's response was chilling: "Yeah, it's over. I ended it."

I was confused. Had I not ended it on the phone with Ethan's dad? Had that conversation not brought resolution to the situation? Why would Kevin say that? So I had to ask, "What does that mean?"

"I told him he better keep your name out of his mouth or I'd punch him in it," Kevin said.

I only remember saying, "Why did you do that?"

Kevin smiled and said, "I'm just getting really sick of people talking about you like that. You're our teacher, and he needs to stop being an asshole."

I didn't know how to react, so I really didn't. Instead, I just said, "Don't fight. I don't want you fighting."

That smile again, and, "I won't fight. As long as I never hear him talking like that about you."

Just like that, he left. He didn't even give me a chance to respond.

Should this have made me question this child? Probably. But this isolated interaction hadn't yet been accompanied by anything else that was odd, so at that moment, I didn't think a thing of it other than that I was beyond embarrassed that this child had so openly discussed my appearance in a swimsuit with at least one other student. That part bothered me. I remember shivering at the thought, and then pushing it down, not allowing myself to consider seriously that anything might be off, or that it might be strange.

*** *** ***

Kevin wasn't a model student, but he was

extremely smart. He truthfully had no business in my regular English 12 class. He should have been taking a higher-level course, but I soon learned that studying was not a hobby of his, that he much preferred his social life and his adventures with friends to sitting down with a book. But he was more than capable of doing the work for my class, and he always got it done.

Only a handful of my students were intelligent enough to get by without studying very hard, and Kevin was one of them. So I encouraged him to channel his superpower into something positive. He did. Casey, a young man who struggled academically but who was one of the nicest humans I've ever met, needed someone like Kevin in his life. Casey struggled to even remember to do his homework, so I made an unusual arrangement with his mother, who lived in my neighborhood: I would leave Casey's homework in my mailbox, and she would pick it up. When he finished, she would return it to my mailbox, and I would take it to school and grade it. We all found out through this that there really are some perks to teaching in a small town, and this was one of them.

I didn't find out until much later that Kevin was the reason why Casey earned his English credit that year. Kevin spent many evenings perched on lawn chairs in the bed of Casey's truck, completing homework as these two teenage boys both worked toward a common goal – graduation.

When Casey would work his grade up to passing, Kevin would walk by my room, high-five me, and say, "We're gonna get this kid a diploma!" and keep walking.

Kevin had a seventh-period study hall, but he wound up spending that time in my classroom almost daily. It was almost like his helping Casey gave him license to adopt my room as his home base, and so he did. He showed up one day during his seventh period and asked to stay. I wrote him a pass, and he never really left after that. It just became what he did until I called the Study Hall monitor to inform him that I would be keeping Kevin permanently during period seven.

For most of the rest of the semester, I saw Kevin every seventh period, and he became my Teacher's Assistant. He adopted the back of my room as his "spot" and he posted himself there daily, waiting for whatever task I had for him. He ran errands, filed papers, and generally took care of the little things that I didn't have time to deal with.

At first, having him in my room during that time was incredibly helpful. But the helpful nature of this arrangement wasn't meant to last, and as time wore on, it began to deteriorate, but not before Kevin, his best friend and I made many memories laughing, joking about life, and at times rolling our eyes about the nuances and the silliness that happens in a school from time to time.

Again, at first, I really loved having him there. The shift happened much later, and it left me with a pit in my stomach and a headache I couldn't explain.

*** *** ***

I remember that first winter well because it was downright frigid outside. It was so cold that we had nine – yes, nine – two-hour delays in a row. I loved those days then, and I still love them now. When school is delayed, I still go in at the regular time, or before, and in two perfect, silent hours, I can accomplish more than I could the entire rest of the day.

Those nine mornings, when my brain was foggy with thoughts of cancer and chemo and when I was so far behind on grading that I couldn't even see my desk, I went in early each day. After about two days of this, Kevin and his best friend caught wind that I was at school early anyway. They asked what I liked from McDonald's, and for seven days in a row, they would show up in my room about an hour before school, toting a bag of greasy breakfast for me plus a Dr. Pepper – my beverage of choice at the time – and they would sit and chat with me while I graded.

We talked about nothing – music, school, college, senior year. There were always other teachers around and our door was always open, but the relationships that developed during those icy mornings felt real, and chatting with them felt so much nicer than worrying about how many more rounds of chemo we had, or whether I could use the pool without scrutiny.

I was smiling about being a teacher for the first time in my short career, all because I had allowed myself a moment of bravery. I poked my head outside my shell, took in the winter air, deemed it safe, and proceeded forward.

I had no clue how wrong I was, and even if someone had told me in those moments what was coming, I'm sure I would never have believed them. Even all these years later, I can say I would still have developed the relationships that I did with those kids.

I still would have taken the risk. But what did I know? I was only 23 years old and had no preparation for what I was about to face.

*** *** ***

Teenagers are perceptive people. They pay attention to more than we think they do, even as they pretend not to care about anything at all. I've learned to be mindful and to watch them watch me over the years. If you look through the scowls and the hair purposefully drawn in front of the eyes, you can pick up on their subtle nuances. It's a very important skill to develop as a teacher.

As I've done this, I've noticed and reacted to so many little changes in my kids, and because I take the time to do this with them, they in turn have done this with me. They react to little things I say when I am teaching, to little jokes I tell, to my subtle changes in personality if I'm having a rough day or if I wake up grouchy. As much as they would have you believe this isn't the case, it absolutely is. They notice their teachers are humans, and they appreciate when teachers don't try to act like they don't also have lives and feelings. It breaks down barriers and paves the way for incredible trust and relationship-building with kids.

One such day like this, Kevin cornered me after class. It was a day that female teacher who had it out for me was really wearing me out. Apparently I wasn't hiding it as well as I thought I was.

"What the hell is going on?" Kevin said.

"I'm not sure what you're talking about," was my reply.

He laughed that laugh: "You know exactly what I'm talking about. You're all 'off' today, so what's going on?"

"Nothing. Grown-up stuff," I said.

Because it was January and he had just had his birthday, he said, "Well, I'm 18. Technically a grownup. So, tell me."

I didn't. "Kevin. Leave it alone. I'm just stressed today. I'm fine."

"OK, sure," he said, "See you tomorrow."

Later that day, Kevin walked by my room while I was talking to my mentor about precisely what was bothering me. We were speaking in hushed tones in the hallway, and Matt was encouraging me to, once again, just let it go. Essentially, the problem was this: Catherine, the teacher next door to me, absolutely hated my guts. She wanted me fired. She hated the closeness that Matt and I had developed. And she was positive, yes, POSITIVE, that my mentor and I had something untoward happening in our relationship.

Obviously, this wasn't true. But she refused to let it go. She was relentless. She presented her concerns as offers of "help" and when I didn't take them, she viewed this as a personal affront, and only increased the level at which she tormented me through my superiors. I couldn't say how many "reports" this woman made to my supervisors during that year, but I know that it was enough to really cause issues – not because they believed her; quite the opposite, really – but because she would not stop.

This, coupled with my mom's chemo, teenagers testing me at every turn and trying to figure out my new life, was simply too much. I was creeping back toward my unhealthy coping mechanisms, and my students, Kevin specifically, were picking up on my retreat.

I guess I revealed that through my facial expressions that day, and, as most kids do, Kevin smelled blood. I did my best to deny any issues – I promise that I did. And I thought our conversation was the end of it.

It wasn't.

*** *** ***

The very next week, my mentor Matt came to me and said, "We have a problem."

"What's that?" I asked.

"Well, Catherine has been receiving some pretty dark, nasty phone calls at home in the evenings."

Incredulous, I said, "What?"

Matt confirmed what he had just said, and then: "Listen, we don't know who is doing this, but we have a pretty good idea. We think it might be Kevin."

My entire body, for the first of many times moving forward that year, was suddenly covered in goosebumps. A chill ran up my spine. I could feel my scalp prickle from this information. At the time, I was completely unable to articulate why. I would have denied to the end that Kevin had anything to do with a prank like this. I would have never pegged him to do this – but then, why wouldn't I have? Was my gut screaming at me for a reason? Was I just feeling these goosebumps on my skin at random? Probably not – goosebumps rarely appear for no reason, but like most painful or difficult things that year, I chose to ignore it.

I think that was the moment when I started to under-stand what I was dealing with. But it wasn't until much later that I was willing to admit that I knew. And maybe the knowing wasn't on a conscious level at that time. Maybe the knowing was buried, deep inside, with my feelings about cancer.

Perhaps I just wasn't willing to face it yet, and so I didn't.

I replied to Matt, "Why on earth would you think it was Kevin?"

"Lindsey, Kevin is a nut job. We think he knows Catherine hates you. And we think he's punishing her for that."

I laughed. I seriously laughed – and now I marvel at how naïve I was to what was happening around me. "Matt, that is ridiculous. That's some serious 'Fatal Attraction' stuff. Absolutely no way."

He said, "I know. But you need to understand that this is getting weird. And you probably need to place some distance between yourself and this kid."

I brushed him off, and dismissed him. And I shouldn't have.

That night, I received a text message from a number I had never seen before.

It was simple: "Hi."

I ignored it.

The next night, another text: "Why don't you answer me?"

I ignored it again.

I knew exactly who was texting me. I knew it was Kevin. I don't know how, but my gut was screaming, and I knew.

Again, chills ran up my spine. Again, my scalp prickled.

Again, I wasn't sure what was happening.

*** *** ***

T he next day at school, Kevin acted like everything was normal. He didn't mention the texts. He just proceeded with his duties as my TA, and never said a word.

For days, I received one text message a day. For days, I ignored them.

Finally, I responded: "Who is this?" Fully aware of who it was, I awaited his response.

My phone dinged: "You know exactly who this is."

I stopped texting at that point. I tossed my phone down, walked away, and didn't reply. I was fairly disturbed by this, but again, chose not to deal with it.

Until the next evening when it happened again.

And again.

This went on for several evenings over the span of a couple of weeks. I responded sporadically, but never anything but messages like, "You need to lose this number," or "Let's just talk at school." I knew this was a problem, but I didn't know how to work through it, and I was sure I would be in trouble, though I had done nothing wrong. In hindsight, I should have run as fast as I could to my principal, or to my mentor, to someone who could help me figure this out, who could help me stop it.

Instead, I pulled in.

Back into my shell I went, distancing myself from Matt, from my colleagues, from everyone. I still talked to Kevin during the school day, and he still acted like nothing weird was happening. I did the same. A couple times, I almost brought up the texting, but I never did. I'm still not sure why. Maybe it was the insane nature of what was happening.

Maybe it was because I wasn't capable myself of believing what I was living. Maybe it was that there is NOTHING in teacher school that prepares a young professional for a situation like this one. In some ways, now, I'm glad, because if this was the kind of struggle teachers had regularly, I wanted nothing to do with it.

I know for certain that once, and once only in a person's career, can a situation like this one arise and be survived.

Not more than that. Just once.

I wasn't the only teacher who received creepy messages from Kevin. I know he called Catherine. His texts to me proved it, and I'm guessing he overheard me talking about Catherine with Matt in the hallway that day. But for some reason, I couldn't bring myself to share that with anyone. My first husband, who was my fiancé at the time and who was also our school resource officer, knew. I told him what was going on, so after a few weeks of this, he insisted that I get my phone number changed. This ended up being a good decision, but it was a futile effort because Kevin somehow quickly gained access to this new phone number as well.

The messages continued. I would respond occasionally, but eventually I stopped altogether. This wound up creating some serious tension between Kevin and me. Suddenly, he was withdrawn, grouchy, and a little short with me. He barely made eye contact with me, and hardly ever smiled. I could tell something was eating away at him, and I think deep down I suspected it was the lack of response he was getting from me, but I never asked and we never discussed it.

*** *** ***

These crazy events somehow became even more strange when my classroom keys went missing. I remember the day well. I knew I was leaving school after seventh period to attend my first bridal appointment with my mom, my sister, and my grandma to choose a wedding gown. It must have been right around the first of April, because I remember that it was still chilly outside and I wore a coat to my appointment.

I was sitting at a student desk – not my own desk – while I was grading and helping students as they worked on group projects. It was seventh period, Kevin was my TA, and I had set my keys on my lesson planning book so I could help a student. I walked over to answer a question, and had my back turned from my things. I wasn't paying attention at all to Kevin, so I didn't see if he walked over and picked up my keys and then resumed his normal activities as if nothing had happened. All I knew was when I looked over at my desk, the keys were gone.

No students saw him, either. If they did, they never reported it to me – or to anyone else.

I felt a lump in my throat and felt tears forming in my eye as I frantically looked all over my room for my keys. Had I dropped them? Did I put them back on my desk? In my bag? What had I done with them?

I knew they were gone, and deep in my gut, I knew what happened. A wise teaching mentor once told me to always keep my classroom keys and my car keys separate from each other in case of a situation like this – this way, I could still go home if somehow my school keys disappeared or were misplaced. I always did that, but when I left school that day, having reported my keys missing to the proper authorities, I felt a void in the pit of my stomach. What had happened? What had I allowed to occur? Who had them?

I knew they were gone and, deep down, I knew who had them.

How did I know Kevin took my keys? I knew the same way I knew he was the one calling Catherine. I knew the same way I knew he was the one texting me. My gut told me. In the weeks leading up to this, I had drawn in more, and I was in total turtle mode. I was leaning less on Matt, and interacting less frequently with my colleagues. I was trying, unsuccessfully, to distance myself from Kevin. It's not like he ever did anything violent or scary to me, or around me. It's not like he ever threatened me, and I knew without a doubt at the time – or I thought I did – that he wasn't going to hurt me. But I also knew that what was happening was totally abnormal and really creepy.

With my keys gone, I felt responsible for the school building. What if something happened, or if there was some act of vandalism? It would all be my fault. I had keys not only to the front doors of the school, but to my own class-room, and even to the pool, too. What if someone snuck in there and drowned? That would be my fault, too, and the guilt was eating me alive. As I tried to smile through my bridal appointment that afternoon, those thoughts crept in, grew stronger, and just made me sick. I hated that this supposedly pivotal life event that I was sharing with the three most important women in my life was being over-shadowed by yet another weird event, which was totally orchestrated by Kevin.

I think it was then that I started to understand exactly

what I was dealing with. I began to look at Kevin differently, to realize that I wasn't dealing with your run-of-the-mill high school senior. Again, clouded by chemo, death, and the daily requirements of first-year teaching, I said nothing. I just pulled further in. I closed my already fairly small circle of people I trusted and interacted with, and I pressed forward.

My administrators assured me that the issue of the missing keys wasn't my fault, that they were taking care of it, and that I didn't need to worry.

I worried anyway. My worry didn't bring my keys back, though.

*** *** ***

This went on for a few weeks, and while I attempted to solve the mystery of the keys and their disappearance, I started to ask questions about Kevin to the people I worked with.

People told various stories of Kevin and their interactions with both him and his parents. The bottom line was this: Some couldn't believe I hadn't had trouble with him, some thought he was weird, and others said that something about him "just didn't seem right." I would relay my claim of having "no issues" with Kevin to them, and they would all stare at me, incredulous, and then usually make a comment like, "Well, you're about the only one."

Maybe I was the only one – or so it seemed – who didn't see Kevin for who he was, or who didn't struggle with him in the classroom the way most teachers did. During this time, I heard some incredible stories, ones that were mostly pretty disturbing.

One specific story stood out more than anything else I had discovered.

When Kevin was in middle school, a friend and fellow teacher told me that he had brought a box to school for her that contained a dead rat. I don't know if it was for scientific purposes – at the time, my friend was a middle school science teacher – but she obviously had no idea what to do with a dead rat in a box. I don't know the ins and outs of how she decided to handle this, but I do know that it involved a parent meeting and, as I learned, this wasn't the first or last time an issue at school prompted a call to Kevin's mom and dad that resulted in some kind of meeting.

My basic understanding of those events was that essentially Kevin's mom and dad were called in to discuss this and other bad behaviors he was exhibiting – chain smoking, disrespect in classrooms, potential drug use – and the rat was just the icing on the proverbial cake. His parents, like his teachers, were at a loss as to what was happening with him. I know it's true that you never really know what goes on behind closed doors in someone's home, and so appearances from the outside are just that – and I really couldn't figure Kevin out.

He was the only child of somewhat older parents who had tried for several years to have him. Mom and Dad were both highly educated, smart, kind people. They still are, I'm sure. I've lost touch with them over the years, but I remember my interactions with them well – always positive, always upbeat, even in times of extreme frustration with whatever odd thing Kevin seemed to be engaged in at the time.

Now that I am a parent, I am aware that it is impossible as a mother to see my child the way other people see him. I am aware there are things about my son that are undesirable to others, but that are invisible to me, and so I empathize with his parents more than I ever have. Like Kevin's parents, I waited a very long time for my son – I suffered years of infertility and wondering if being a mom was ever going to be possible for me, and so I really do feel that on some level, I can appreciate his parents' approach to child-rearing.

But I also know that one of my primary goals in life is to raise young men who are positive contributors to society and who bring love and light wherever they go. I think at times, I take for granted that this is my goal in parenting, and that it is not the goal of every other parent. And so, while I empathize on a level I never could have before my son Andrew was born, I still cannot understand, and maybe never will, what happened to make Kevin the person he was when I knew him.

*** *** ***

About a week after I started my fact-finding mission about Kevin, the mystery of the keys still had not been solved. School administrators were thinking it might be time to involve the police, and since my fiancé was the police at my school, we talked quite often about this at home. He urged me to continue to distance myself from Kevin – I'm not sure either of us could pinpoint exactly what our "bad" feelings were, but we knew we both had them.

It was around this time that Karl, our assistant principal and someone who had started to become a friend that year, visited me in my room. We stepped out to talk.

"Hey, Linds. I think we have a lead on the keys," he said.

The conversation was happening in the hallway, as my students worked independently in my classroom.

"Really?" I asked, hopeful.

"Yeah, but it's weird," he answered.

Those goosebumps again: "What do you mean?"

"Well, we got a call from Kevin."

Now, I was confused: "Kevin?"

"Yes. He claims he can get the keys back," Karl said.

"Oh, great!" I responded. But then I remembered I was sure Kevin was the one who took them in the first place, so I said, "But wait ..."

Karl said, "Right. That's why it's weird."

"So, how is he going to get them back if he's the one who took them?" I asked.

Karl laughed. "That's a pretty good question," he said. "He also has some conditions."

Now I was really freaked out. My scalp prickled again. "Conditions?"

"Yeah, he made us promise we wouldn't involve the authorities if he could return the keys," Karl said.

"Wait. What?"

"Right. He's decided that striking a deal with us is the way to go here," Karl said.

He chuckled a little, and I felt myself pull in, just a little more, away from this person and from all of the other people. In my head, I said, "What is happening?" But no answers came.

As we worked through the details of this, I felt myself zone out. I occasionally peeked in at the students in my room. They were working along, doing normal teenage things in a normal school. And I was standing out in a hallway, separated from my normal by a door and a wall and a kid who, no matter how hard I tried, kept pulling me as far away from regular life as he possibly could. Later, much later, I would understand that all of this was intentional, and carefully calculated. But at that time, I was incapable.

As I tuned back in to what Karl was saying, I registered his final words to me: "Lindsey, this is getting serious, and it's getting weird, and I need you to promise me that you'll stop talking to this kid. I really need you to create some distance. No matter how he reacts. DO NOT allow him to get to you."

Chills again.

"OK," I said, "So, what do I do about seventh period?" Kevin was in my room two periods a day. How could I distance myself in this situation?

"We are going to just ask that you do your best. I know this is hard, Linds, but things are getting weird, and we need to keep you safe."

"I understand," I said. But I really didn't. My head was spinning. Safe? How could I not be safe? This kid was a teenager. He was a kid, for crying out loud. How could he possibly be dangerous or harmful to me?

I didn't know in that moment, but I would soon find out just how harmful my bosses thought he could potentially be.

As I walked back in to the normalcy of my classroom, I felt myself exhale for the first time since this conversation had begun. On the bright side, my keys would be returned. On the weird side, I had no idea what was transpiring in the main office about this suddenly serious situation.

My conversation with Karl jarred me back to reality and, at the very least, it allowed me to give a name to what I was feeling: Fear. I was afraid. Of what, I was not exactly sure. Or maybe it was whom. I didn't know. My head was so jumbled, my thoughts so scattered, that I was incapable of grabbing onto any specific thought or reason. I just knew I didn't feel right, and in retrospect, I hadn't for some time.

Upon reflection, I had pushed away any feelings of unease about Kevin over and over again, until it became commonplace for me to ignore little, unnerving things that under normal circumstances – or if I had more experience as a teacher – would have caused me to pause and talk to someone about what I was witnessing.

*** *** ***

Distancing myself from Kevin, for me, meant less of everything – less talking, less interacting, less eye contact. All of it. It was difficult, but I knew that the distance had to be created, that it was important to ending whatever was going on. Kevin, though, was not fooled by anything I did or did not say. He noticed every subtle change I made. And he asked me about all of them.

"What the hell? You haven't talked to me in three days," I remember him saying.

"I don't know what you're talking about," I replied.

"That's bullshit. And you know it," he said, "I've been so stressed, and I haven't even been able to talk to you about it because you keep ignoring me."

There was the guilt again. He was trying to make me

feel it, and it was working. "Kev..." I said.

"I'm just freaking out a little bit," he shared.

"Why are you freaking out?"

"Well," he said, "I'm just not super sure about college. Like what I want to do, where I want to go, all of it. It's overwhelming."

I totally understood that: "I get it. I know it can be like that. So, what are you thinking you want to study?" I asked him.

"Well, probably pharmacy," he answered.

I chuckled, and for once it was me laughing and not him: "So, you're planning to take this drug-dealing enterprise of yours to the legal side of things?"

He blushed, literally the first time I had ever thrown him off with anything I said, and then he returned my laugh: "Yeah, I guess you could say that."

"Kevin, everything is going to work out fine. You're plenty smart enough to be successful in a pharmacy program. I know you are," I said. And I believed this. He was very smart – way too smart, in fact.

But in that moment, all I saw was a scared, intimidated kid – almost like a little boy – trying to figure out the ins and outs of college applications and working through all of the other tedious details that can make a senior year very busy and intimidating. I celebrated internally for a second – he was talking about his future, about normal teenage concerns, and he was doing it with what I thought was the utmost sincerity.

I didn't understand at the time that this conversation was probably a distraction, a way to move my mind to something else, to think of him in terms of the future and how it was going to play out for him. It just felt like the first normal conversation we'd had in weeks, and I remember enjoying what I thought was "regular" Kevin.

I didn't find out until later that "regular" Kevin was an idea that I made up in my mind. He didn't really exist – the only Kevin that existed was the real, actual kid.

The only Kevin was the one standing in front of me with more going on in his brain than I ever could have – or still can – imagine.

The only Kevin was the one who I recognize now as the instrument of my needing a whole bunch of help with my own coping skills as a grown adult.

And this one Kevin was the one who taught me the meaning of the phrase "once-in-a-lifetime," just not in the way most people learn it.

5

Chapter

'We Think He's Going to Do Something Weird'

The last morning of my first life began just as every morning since the previous August had, with a five o'clock alarm that jarred me from sleep. I stumbled to the shower, rubbing my eyes and trying to establish some coherence in my thoughts for the day.

It was April 19, 2007, and I had been teaching for a little over eight months. I wouldn't say I was good at what I was doing just yet, but at least I had acclimated much better to the routine. My brain was still foggy, but as my mom's chemo treatments had ended and her hair had started to grow back, I was feeling more normal than I had for a really long time. The brain fog had started to lift, the weather outside was warming up, I had agreed to marry a man I thought I loved, and life just felt like it had more purpose than it had before.

I felt good, really good, for the first time in what seemed like forever.

I had no idea that this was the last day I would wake

up feeling like this for a seriously long time. I had no way of knowing that this was the last day of my life that I would ever wake up as the person I was that morning.

Immediately at the sound of the alarm, just like they had every day until this one, my thoughts jumped to my school checklist. Teachers make thousands of decisions every day, and that decision-making streak begins early and lasts far beyond the end of the school day. I finished dressing – I had learned what it meant to make myself look like a grownup – so the stress of what to wear in the morning had diminished slightly. What had not changed at all was the routine: waking up every day with my mind racing, and heading to school as early as possible to try to get everything figured out before the students arrived.

My arrival to school that day was also standard. I drove the short distance from home to school, parked my car, and began another day of business as usual. I had no reason to think or feel that this day would be different from all of the other days in any substantial way. At that juncture, there was no way for me to know just how wrong I was.

The day passed in relative normalcy. I taught my six classes, interacted with kids and joked with colleagues. I avoided Kevin, just as I had for the three weeks or so between my last conversation with Karl, my assistant principal, and this day. I had learned nothing more about the retrieval of the missing keys, and as such, I assumed they had been returned to administration. I got a new classroom key, and I never saw those old keys again.

And then one phone call began the longest 48 hours of my life.

It was Thursday – a little before the end of the school

day – and the voice on the other end of the line of my classroom phone belonged to Jenny French, the director of our Guidance Office.

"Hey, Lindsey. We need you to come down at the end of the day today for a meeting," she said.

"A meeting?" I asked, very curious.

"Yes. We need to see you and all of Kevin's teachers before you leave school today. Please don't do anything else after the bell. Just come straight here."

For the remaining minutes of seventh period, I pushed down some serious feelings of doubt, worry, and frankly, nausea. I wasn't sure what they wanted to talk about, and yet I knew that it was gravely serious by the tone of Jenny's voice when she called me. Kevin was right there in my room – and he apparently watched the color drain from my face while I talked on the phone.

He took it upon himself to ask me about it.

"Why is your face literally gray?" he asked.

"Is it?" I returned the question.

"Yeah. You look terrible," he said.

"I'm just not feeling great. My stomach is upset," was my reply.

Kevin walked away then, and I didn't speak to him for the rest of the day. As instructed, when the bell rang and the students cleared out of my room, I made my way to Jenny's office for our meeting.

The relatively short walk to the main office dragged as I let my brain fill with worry and fear about what they wanted to discuss. More than once, I wondered if somehow the missing keys and the creepy text messages were finally going to cause my administrators to shift their support away from me. I sure hoped not, but the thought of Kevin's causing them to turn their backs on me did cross my mind. But then, why would they want to talk to all of his teachers if they had an issue to address with me?

Common sense took over then, and I realized that this was much bigger than anything that dealt exclusively with me.

I was right.

I entered the office last. My walk was the longest, so the rest of Kevin's teachers had already arrived and were waiting for me before we were filled in on what was happening. Jenny closed the door and took a seat at her desk, and Jane Berensen, the principal, was already standing in a corner of Jenny's office.

She started talking, and as she spoke, I felt my vision tunnel, my scalp prickle, and my body cover itself in goose-bumps. I don't remember every word she said, but, loud and clear, I heard, "Listen, we think he is going to do something weird. And we think it's going to be tomorrow."

"Weird?" I heard myself asking, unable to stop myself. If it's possible, I could feel the gray in my face once again – if a person can physically feel color drain from one's face, I felt it in that moment.

Jenny responded: "Yes. Like violent weird. And we aren't sure you're safe."

"Who isn't safe?" I asked.

"Well, you," she answered, "Everyone else, too. But mostly you. And Kaitlyn." I looked to the other side of the room then, and saw Kaitlyn, Kevin's counselor, sitting in the corner, equally horrified, but not nearly as surprised as I was.

If there was anyone in the building who was closer to Kevin than I was, it was Kaitlyn. She was his counselor and had worked with him for three years, so she did know him a little better than I did, and she understood his little nuances better than most people. Kaitlyn and I had a few short conversations about him over the previous several months, but not many. We weren't terribly close at the time of this meeting, but like most things in life, what Kevin was planning had some unintended consequences, and Kaitlyn's becoming my best friend was meant to be long before either she or I knew we'd be on that path. We were unaware the cards that had to fall in order for this to happen, at least at the time, but I think we would both say now that we are thankful to have had each other in the days, weeks, and months following this meeting in Jenny's office.

It was obvious she already knew what this meeting was about, that she already knew what they thought was going to happen the following day.

This information created more questions than it answered, but at the time I wasn't given the chance to answer them. Instead, his teachers were filled in on the plan for how we would get through the next day, the measures the school was taking to keep the student body safe, and how we were to handle conversations with Kevin, should they arise.

Essentially, our administrators thought they had reason to believe that Kevin had plans to engage in some sort of violent act at school the following day. I never learned what their real reasoning was, or the actual tipping point for the decisions they made, but in that meeting, it was shared with us that the following day in school, we would notice a tremendous increase in police presence. Our instructions were to proceed as normal through our school day, and if Kevin asked us about the policemen, we were to play dumb.

Meeting adjourned.

Except for me.

They asked me to stay a minute after the meeting. I remained in my seat as the rest of Kevin's teachers filed out. Still unsure how to process what was being said to me, I didn't speak or move. I couldn't, so I just waited.

Jane spoke first: "Lindsey, when we told you what we thought was going to happen, all of the color drained from your face. Are you OK?"

"I think so," I said.

Jane again: "Did you have any idea that he was planning something?"

Incredulous, I said, "Absolutely not. I haven't really spoken to him in weeks."

"We just think there's a chance, especially with you and Kaitlyn, that he will have some sort of 'I'm going to take you with me' mentality, and this is the only way we know how to prevent that," Jane said, trying to reassure me. "But when all the color drained – you turned WHITE – I got worried."

"I'm fine. This is just scary," I answered.

"I know. But we will keep you safe," Jane said.

I really appreciated that, but I didn't feel reassured at all. I just felt sick. What was this kid planning? What was he capable of? And why in the world did it have anything to do with me? And what was I supposed to do now? How does a person just go on with her day when she possesses information like this?

I had no answer for that. I left school in a fog that day, shaking.

*** *** ***

I wish I could remember precisely what happened between the end of school and having dinner at home with my fiancé that night, but I can't. I am sure I fixed dinner, cleaned up, and maybe even did a little bit of laundry – and I'm sure I did everything within my power to be "normal," though I felt anything but "normal."

I know I asked my fiancé, a police officer, what to expect the next day. Scott was our School Resource Officer at the time, and if anyone could answer this question, it would be him. But I don't think he knew, either. Neither of us had ever been a part of something like this.

He just said, "Listen. Lock your room, don't let anyone in, and stay away from that kid the best you can."

I know Scott was frustrated by the whole situation because he was the one who had been charged with the task of hiring the extra officers and coordinating when they would be at school, and what they would do while they were there. This was no easy task, and I remember him being annoyed with filling time slots, explaining the situation to the officers, and trying to figure out how to keep a building of over a thousand kids safe from one of their own.

Thankfully, the time slots were all filled, and the officers were scheduled. We all knew our roles as we walked into this Friday of uncertainty. We just didn't know that Kevin, as per his usual pattern of behavior, would surprise us. We didn't know what he was planning, and some parts of me wonder if he even completely knew how it was going to unfold.

But it unfolded – not like we thought it would, thankfully – but instead in a way that left all of us reeling. In that way, I am sure it all went according to plan. Kevin always was one for craving attention, with something of a flair for the dramatic.

He sure lived up to his personality in the 24 hours that followed – and none of our lives were ever the same.

Chapter

Don't Let Him
Out of Your Sight

The thought of not going to school on Friday, April 20 never crossed my mind – though in hindsight, I have asked myself a hundred times why not. I wish I had the answer to that question. If a person was in danger in a specific place – or even in potential danger – why wouldn't she just not go to that place?

I think I went to school that Friday because part of me doubted the legitimacy of what had been said to me just 12 hours before. After all, I worked at one of the highest per-forming school districts in the Indianapolis area. We had GOOD kids that came from GOOD families who just simply didn't do things like this. The fear that Kevin was going to commit an act of mass violence that day was a real one – the fear that he was going to hurt himself and take Kaitlyn and I with him was real, too. It was never far from my mind that day, but I think I was in somewhat of a state of denial, as I refused to acknowledge that I was in danger – surely this was not going to happen to me – and as I attempted to will it into reality, preparations were being made all over school in the event that I was the one who was wrong.

I could not wrap my head around the idea, and in true turtle fashion, I chose to ignore it as much as I possibly could.

And so, to school I went.

Arriving at school wasn't much different than it had been any other day – minus the influx of police cars lining the front of the building and the excessive number of uniformed men patrolling the halls. Because I was engaged to a police officer, men in uniform were not at all unfamiliar to me, but having so many of them walking the hallways of our building was not the norm – and I knew people would notice – in truth, I knew Kevin would notice.

And I knew he wouldn't let it go.

I was right.

My morning passed as normal – minus the pit in my stomach that had formed the night before and continued to grow as time passed.

When I reflect on the events of that day, and I think of the day from start to finish, time always slows to a nauseating crawl. Many of the details of April 20 – what I wore, who I talked to, what I had for lunch – all of those things are fuzzy. What I do remember is that time was not my friend that day. I wanted the day to be over.

I wanted my administration to be wrong.

Oh, how I wanted them to be wrong.

I taught my first two or three classes as normal. Finally, it was my prep period, and I had a moment to breathe. I needed to run to the office to check my mailbox, so I opened my classroom door and headed that way. My classroom, located in the English wing, was one of the farthest from the main office, and because I didn't want to encounter too many people that day, I took the "back way."

My school had one hallway that is different from all the rest because it's not lined with classrooms or lockers. Instead, the walls are nearly floor-to-ceiling windows, and it is on an incline. It's part of the original high school building and has survived I don't know how many renovations. I remember it well because it is a distinctive feature of the building, one that I have not seen in any school I have visited or worked in since. But on this day, it created for me a memory I will never forget.

On April 20, I watched the sunlight pour in through those windows as I walked behind two armed policemen I didn't know. I knew why they were there, and I watched them talking to each other ever-so-casually, like nothing was wrong. In that moment, they weren't specifically protecting me – in fact, I'm not sure they even knew I was watching them. But they were protecting everyone else – making their rounds carefully, ensuring nothing was amiss. The tools and weapons on their belts gleamed in the sunlight, rattling with the motion of their walking. There to remind me that this was anything but a normal day, I remember watching their feet shuffle in unison down the slanted hallway – I think one of them even laughed – and as they did this, I felt the pit in my stomach grow again.

What was I doing here?

What were they doing here?

Surely this was all a dream, a false alarm. Right?

On a normal day, I might have said hello to those officers – I would have known them; they would have known me. They would have had some sort of joke for me, and I would have reciprocated. On any other day, I might have walked through the halls with them, talking and visiting through some or all of my prep period.

But I can't tell you why I didn't talk to them that day. Something felt different – something was very different. Maybe this was how I acknowledged that – by NOT acknowledging it. But I kept being reminded that this was far from a normal day – that nagging pit in my stomach would not dissipate, and I could not shake the thought of how Kevin might react if he knew exactly what those officers were doing there.

Truth be told, I think this was the first time I was able to admit to myself that I felt fear at what was to come, or what was potentially to come, in the hours of the day that lay ahead of us.

*** *** ***

It was almost lunch, and I still hadn't seen Kevin at all. I remember wondering if he'd even come to school, as Mondays and Fridays were his favorite days to miss, and he did so with some frequency. But Kevin was quite the showman – and I doubted that he would miss an opportunity to be the center of attention.

I was right.

Just as I thought that maybe he didn't come to school at all that day, there he was.

He opened my classroom door – presumably on his way to lunch, because that's where I was headed, and he would be coming to my class directly after we ate. The conversation we had then will be forever seared into my memory. He didn't come all the way into the room at that time – he just peeked his head through a small-ish crack between the door and its frame, cocked his head to one side, and said, "Hey. What are all these cops doing here?"

I obviously couldn't and wouldn't answer him with the truth, so I said, "I have no idea."

His response is something that, thirteen years later, I can still hear:

"You're a fucking liar," he said.

He slammed the door and he was gone.

While this conversation disturbed me, I didn't allow myself to become fixated on analyzing why. Instead, I attempted, the best I could, not to allow his venom to bother me. Many times, I had seen this side of him directed at other people – this was the first time he had ever turned on me, and to say it wasn't disturbing and a little scary would be a lie.

Kevin came to class after lunch and didn't speak to me. He never looked at me once – never made eye contact. As the bell rang to end class, he shuffled out with the rest of my seniors, and didn't acknowledge that I was even in the room. Staying focused on distancing myself from him, I assume this was what I should have wanted, but I found myself more disturbed than anything else, as this was so far from what I had grown accustomed to.

For Kevin to ignore me was so strange and outside the norm that I had no clue how to handle it. And I know he was just a kid, but something about his demeanor was just icy and distant. It's hard to explain, but this wasn't the kind of distant that most people have experienced. This distant was permanent, a separation. From any other 18-year-old kid,

I would not have thought twice, and I definitely would not have questioned what was happening. But as I learned to face the truth about Kevin, I learned that he was definitely having some serious mental health issues. Nothing he did was without purpose. Nothing he did was without careful calculation. And nothing he did was without several strings attached for whomever chose to take his help or to step into his influence in some way. And so, his ignoring me was more than that – it was eerie and somewhat frightening, but at the time, I had no way of explaining why or how.

*** *** ***

The school day ended, for me, uneventfully. The "take you with me" situation that my administration feared would be our reality that day appeared to have not come true. And when the bell rang to end the school day, I found myself breathing a sigh of relief – completely unaware that some of the longest hours of my life were still ahead of me – completely unaware that on the other side of the building, in Kevin's counselor's office, the battle to keep him alive was just beginning.

I learned much later that Kaitlyn's job was to keep Kevin with her at the end of the day, presumably to prevent him from having access to a large group of people where he could potentially wreak havoc in the final minutes of the school day. Because Kevin wasn't stupid, Kaitlyn knew that she would have to come up with a logical, plausible reason to need to talk with him, and as we were five weeks from graduation, she had one: college.

For years after this series of events, Kaitlyn and I had

conversations about Kevin and what transpired in those weeks of that first school year we spent together. We went around and around the events of that year over and over again, and always, her conversation with him at the end of school on Friday, April 20 is one of the most bone-chilling conversations I've ever had relayed to me.

Kaitlyn's meeting with Kevin was largely successful: she avoided his having access to a large crowd at dismissal; she contained him in one place on a Friday afternoon; her ruse of talking about college was believable. But the end of the conversation is what, all these years later, still hasn't left me.

When the conversation was over, Kaitlyn looked at Kevin and said, "I'll see you Monday."

Mirroring the interaction I had with him earlier that day, Kevin was halfway out Kaitlyn's office door when she said this to him. And as he replied, he peered around the edge of her door frame and said, "You won't see me Monday, Ms. Gatewood."

And with a smile, he left.

*** *** ***

The rest of how that day was handled and by whom isn't totally clear to me, and I'm not sure that it needs to be. My basic understanding of the rest of that afternoon and evening sort of stops when I left school. I mean, I survived, right? It was over.

Little did I know that the horror was just beginning.

One thing I do know was that Kaitlyn called Kevin's mom at the end of the school day. I know everyone was relieved that nothing weird happened during school that day, but the thought that Kevin was suicidal or that he might hurt other people was still a very real one, and one that, despite the relative uneventful nature of that school day, could not be ignored. In that phone conversation, Kaitlyn told Kevin's mom:

"Whatever you do, do NOT let him out of your sight."

Kaitlyn was assured this would be the case, and so I think we all went home feeling confident that we had done everything we could to keep Kevin – and the rest of the high school staff and students – safe.

Some of the details of that day might be fuzzy, but one thing that isn't was the memory I have of breathing a sigh of exhausted relief as I started my car to go home at the end of the day. Relief that Kevin hadn't hurt anyone mixed well with exhaustion, and I had trouble wading through those feelings, but I remember thinking specifically that the incident they all predicted was going to occur that day had not come true, and so I was out of the woods. Or so I thought.

But as the next 12 hours unfolded, I remember thinking – and for several months after that day, I continued to think – that I wished I had never met Kevin.

I wished I had never allowed him to suck me in the way he did, to fool me into believing that he was just a normal kid. Or to make me believe somehow that he was capable of having my – or anyone else's – best interest at heart.

But I learned that day – and I learned even more as the whole truth was revealed in the weeks that followed – that Kevin was far from normal.

7

Chapter

The Calm Before The Storm

By the time I get to Friday at the end of a school week, I always feel the same: exhausted, totally spent, and like I can't possibly do one more thing. This has been true since the beginning of my career and is still true today – most Friday nights in my house look like pajamas before 7 p.m. and a pizza. We usually turn in early, and we make very little effort to leave the house. It's a tradition that I have grown to absolutely love.

By Friday – every week – I've potentially had nearly one thousand conversations, and that's only if I speak to each student only one time per day each week. That doesn't include adults, phone calls, people who aren't in my class, or emails. It definitely doesn't include the papers I've graded or the meetings I've attended. And that's just at school. Let's not even get into the responsibilities I have at home with two growing boys, a husband, a house and two pets. By the end of the week, all of this human interaction takes quite the emotional toll, and I'm usually looking for as quiet a

Friday night as I can muster. I'm sure if your world is at all similar to mine, Friday looks quite a bit like that for you, too.

Friday, April 20, 2007, was no exception. I wasn't a mother back then, so I had the luxury of going home, napping if I wanted to – I always wanted to – eating a slow, relaxed dinner, and heading to bed early. Even as a 23-year-old, fresh out of college with plenty of social invitations, all I really wanted to do was go home. And stay home.

After the events of that day – after dodging the bullet I thought we had dodged – that's exactly what I did.

I am sure that I sat down with my fiancé at some point, too – I remember he was working a security detail somewhere else that night, so he was only able to stop home for dinner briefly, but in that brief conversation, we talked through and processed many of that day's events.

I remember asking him how he felt about the day – and him sort of brushing it off. Police officers have an odd compartmentalization strategy they use in their lives to put things to bed once they're over. They don't dwell much; they don't overthink, and they certainly don't "what-if" a situation to death. These are all things, however, that I do extremely well. And that night, I wanted to.

"What do you think really would have happened today?" I asked him.

He replied, "I don't know. But it didn't happen, so we are going to just be lucky for that."

I knew he was right, but I couldn't let it go. "Do you think he even owns a gun? Like a real, actual gun?"

Scott said, "Honey, I don't know. All I know is that I hired some extra guys for today, they did their jobs, and now the day is over."

And with that, Scott returned to his security detail and we didn't talk again until the following morning. I was fast asleep by the time he got home well after midnight. Knowing me, I wasn't able to fully let it go, but in the absence of someone with whom to process my thoughts, I went to bed, knowing that we had somehow survived one of our toughest days yet.

*** *** ***

During this time period, my sister, who lived and worked in Southern Indiana, frequently came to my house on Friday nights to stay. She liked being in Indy for the weekends, and my house was a really good halfway point between her place down south and her boyfriend's house. Many weekends were spent holed up at my place, just the four of us – we made some amazing memories together during this time period.

This Friday night was the beginning of another one of these weekends, and I knew my sister was on her way as I settled myself into bed for the night. Lauren had a key to the house, so I didn't worry about her ability to get in or to find her bed once she was inside. This was a normal part of the routine.

She arrived late – after 11:30 – and I was absolutely asleep. But that night, my sister did something she had never done before. She woke me up.

Our bedroom door had a tendency to stick, and the noise from her opening it woke me before her voice. The door was shoved open with a thud, and then: "Linds, something serious is going on outside your neighborhood," she said.

"What?" I responded in a fog.

"I just had to take the back way in because the other entrance is completely blocked," she said.

"By what?" I asked.

"It looks like a bunch of police cars and ambulances and I think a couple fire trucks, too. It looks like there might have been a really bad wreck."

"Are you OK?" I remember asking her.

"Yeah, I'm fine. But someone isn't," she said. "I'm going to bed."

We said good night then, and I quickly went back to sleep, thinking nothing of our conversation other than a sigh of relief that my sister was safe.

*** *** ***

When I was young and capable of sleeping in, I did just that on Saturday mornings. On most Saturdays, I didn't rise before nine, and on this Saturday, April 21, was no different. My eyes opened slowly, and I found myself reluctant to extract my tired body from the comfort of my bed. Curled up next to me was my dog – she loved to sandwich herself in the middle of the bed, take over half my pillow, and snore all night long. She made no exceptions this day, and as I roused myself from sleep, I reached for the phone, which was next to the bed.

I'd heard it buzz a couple of times as I was waking up, but until this point, had ignored the noise. But as I slid it open, I realized it had buzzed far more than I originally thought. It took me a minute to register the five missed calls and ten or more text messages from various fellow teachers. I couldn't locate any details, but from the tone of the "Call me as soon as you get this" messages, it didn't take me long to figure out that something was very wrong.

First on the list of people to call back: my mentor, Matt.

As I started to dial his number, Scott's phone also started to go crazy. I stopped what I was doing in that moment to allow him to answer. Pausing my call to Matt gave me many of the answers I needed in that moment. A fellow police officer was on the line.

I could tell that what he was saying was tremendously difficult – Scott's reaction was shock, and as he hung up the phone, I knew that what he was about to say to me was not going to be easy.

Scott collected himself for a minute and then said, "Honey, there's been an accident."

"OK," I replied.

"Kevin is dead," he said.

Chapter

Prom

Dead? How could Kevin be dead?

How did this happen? When did this happen?

The confusion swirled around me as I attempted to make sense of what I was being told, and as I started to process and comprehend Scott's words, a tear fell from my eye. I felt it run down my face, followed by another, and another – no full-fledged sobbing, no waterfall of tears, just a steady stream.

I know that policemen are trained to make notifications to loved ones of deceased people and that they do this all the time. I know, also, that their training tells them to be quick and direct in their notifications – and that is exactly what Scott did in the moment, temporarily forgetting I was his fiancé, that I knew Kevin well, and that I was in danger not 24 hours before – because of Kevin.

Momentarily shocked by his lack of sensitivity, I said, "Kevin who?"

"Kevin. The only Kevin we know. He and two friends were in a wreck on our road last night, and he didn't make it."

"What do you mean he didn't make it? What three kids? What are you talking about?" I asked, in rapid fire succession.

"Honey, Kevin and two of his friends left this neighborhood in a car last night. They drove into a tree, and Kevin did not survive the accident," he explained.

I felt my body tingle – the same chills that had gone up my spine and along my scalp for so many months with situations related to Kevin returned, this time more intensely – and the tears started to fall even harder.

"You mean, he's dead?" I asked.

"Yes. He is dead," Scott answered.

I don't know how I moved through the rest of my morning other than that I can track it by phone call: first our principal, Jane. She called to make sure I was OK. Then my mentor, Matt. He also called to see if I had heard – but he was also ensuring that I was OK. Several other colleagues called to check on me. That was their constant question. I have learned over the years that fellow teachers and administrators stop checking on you at a certain point, and as I've grown older and into a more experienced teacher, the checks are less and less, and the concern for my well-being, if it exists, is not expressed nearly as often as it should be. I wish I had known in that moment to be grateful, but all I could focus on was the tunnel-vision grief that was settling into my heart.

The short answer – to all of them – was that I was far from OK.

I learned from Scott, from my colleagues, and from some of the policemen who had worked the crash scene the night before that Kevin and two friends had left our neighborhood, that they had been traveling at a high rate of speed, and that they somehow veered off the road, crashing, driver's side first, into a large tree at the bottom of a driveway.

One of Kevin's friends walked away from the crash with some minor injuries.

Another of Kevin's friends was gravely, critically injured – his prognosis was not good.

And Kevin was killed on impact.

So, no, I was not OK. This was the easy answer to the question posed to me over and over again that morning as I made and received countless phone calls.

But the complicated answer, and the one I still grapple with today is – as not OK as I was, I was also somewhat unsurprised that Kevin had died.

I'm not sure if I had internalized what was being said to me about what could potentially happen or if I just knew, somewhere deep within, that Kevin was not meant for this world. Even years later, I know in my soul that this outcome was the only one we were going to have. That this was the way it was going to end because he made sure of it. The morbidity of that thought is not lost on me.

Even thirteen years later, as I type these words, the chills return to my spine when I think of the gravity of what I just wrote. When I consider that the loss of another human life – a human life that was so young and potentially awaited such a bright future – could bring me what I can now admit was somewhat of a sigh of relief, I have processed and grappled with more guilt than I can express.

In the throes of all of the strange things that happened: the keys, the threatening of kids, the harassment of teachers – all of it – in the middle of all that, it often felt like it was never going to end, that there was no way out. For any of us – and for a moment, the thought crossed my mind that maybe he did this out of fear. Maybe he did this because he also felt trapped in a circular interaction with the situations he had created at school. Maybe, just maybe, some of this was my fault.

As I ruminated on those thoughts, I realized that none of the answers I was seeking would be provided for me that day. Instead, I knew – consciously or otherwise – that the day, and my life, still had to move forward.

And so, I did what all teachers do – I tried to move forward despite my own feelings of grief, confusion, and fear. Kevin was never too far from my mind, and I replayed every interaction with him over and over in my mind as I began to get ready for my day. Memories of Kevin mixed with thoughts of the rest of the student body, and I realized that not every student at our school would have a connection to Kevin, and that some would not even know who he was. For them, this day would proceed as normal – they would expect to continue as if nothing happened, because for them, nothing did happen.

April 21 was supposed to be a happy day for our kids – they would be attending prom that night at our local children's museum, and as a teacher of mostly upper classmen, it had already been in my plan to attend the event. It was the social event of the year for these kids, and the show would still go on, regardless of the storm that was brewing in so many of our hearts and minds that day. It was still our responsibility to provide lifelong memories for students, no matter how sad or distraught we might have been.

Not long after the flood of phone calls from colleagues and police officers stopped, I realized that I had nothing to wear to the prom, and that I had not yet told my mom the news of Kevin's death.

I picked up the phone to call her, and to the best of my ability, relayed what had occurred.

"I'll be there in five minutes," she said.

And she was.

*** *** ***

It was April, and my mom had finished treatment for her cancer that winter – her hair was just starting to grow back in, and our family was finally entertaining the thought of a collective sigh of relief as we did our best to return to some normalcy in our lives. In the months since her diagnosis, Scott and I had gotten engaged, bought a home, moved in together, begun planning a wedding, and started to look forward to a life together. The end of her treatment signaled our planning for the future with her as part of it.

Moving five minutes from where I grew up was never really in my plan, but at the time, it made more sense than anything else. Scott was a police officer in our town, limiting the scope of where we could live, and having ready access to my family was important to me. The fact that I worked at the high school also contributed to our decision, and on this April day, I found it to be a particular blessing that I could just call up sobbing and my mom could be to me in under ten minutes.

When she arrived at my house that day, I don't remember exactly what I said, but the news of the crash came tumbling out of my mouth in a jumbled heap of tears, snot, and garbled language. Because moms are experts on their own children – even the grown ones, she was able to pick through my verbal disaster and discern exactly what had happened.

"You mean, he drove that car into a tree? With other kids in it?" she asked me.

"Yes. Right out there. Last night," I said, pointing in the general direction of the main road on which the accident had occurred.

"And he's dead?" she asked.

"Yes," I said, "He is dead. Apparently. Scott said he didn't make it ... he died on impact."

"Oh my God," she replied.

"I know," I answered.

We sifted through more details of the accident after that, mostly unable to comprehend all that we knew had occurred. What we arrived at, though, was that I still had to face the rest of my students – to be there for them in their time of need. I still had to put on a happy face, show up at the prom, and make sure that the ones who needed hugs got them, and the ones that needed smiling pictures with their friends or with their English teacher got those. I would be playing dual roles that evening, and I needed to figure out how to do that – and quickly.

I spent the afternoon with my mom, processing my feelings, crying occasionally, but really not saying much. We went to lunch at a local restaurant where I ate almost nothing, said almost nothing, and spent nearly the whole time staring off into space.

"Honey, I'm so sorry," my mom said.

"Mom, I just do not understand," I said, "I don't understand how we got here. How we went from stolen keys to he's dead."

Little did I know this thought would be one I returned

to several times over the coming months and years, that this thought would be the cornerstone of what I knew in my soul, and what I learned about what had occurred with Kevin and the circumstances surrounding his death.

I waded through the afternoon, lunching, crying, shopping, and theorizing with my mom, who – bless her soul – listened to the same thoughts over and over as I processed them again and again and tried, desperately, to come to terms with Kevin's death in some peaceful way.

I know now that I was not destined for peace in my heart that day – or in any day in the near future, for that matter – but the circular nature of my thoughts kept my mind at least somewhat occupied as I prepared to put on a happy face for my students at the prom that night.

*** *** ***

Indianapolis has a beautiful children's museum – in fact, it's somewhat world-renowned, and people come from all over the United States and other countries to see what they have on exhibit. The museum also hosts events like weddings, receptions, galas, and, of course, proms. Our school's prom was being held there in 2007, and our students were buzzing with excitement over the venue's beauty and layout – and of course they were buzzing about the usual prom things: dresses, tuxes, and dates were hot topics of conversation in the weeks leading up to the event.

So, for the kids who didn't know Kevin well or at all, April 21 was simply prom day for them. Originally, I had offered to help the prom committee set up for the event – because just two days before, I was a different person than the one I became on this day. I was one of the people who was just going to the prom because it was prom. Two days ago, I wasn't a person who had experienced a life-changing event. Two days ago, I had never been in danger in a school before. Two days ago, I had no idea that I would spend this day questioning the circumstances surrounding this accident, grasping for a why.

But here I was, and at the time, I had no way of understanding that I was permanently changed by this event, only that it brought a numbness to my emotions and to how I moved through the rest of that day and that evening.

As promised, I arrived early to set up and decorate. Much of the work was already done, and everywhere I looked or tried to work, I encountered a person who wanted to know how I was doing. There was no table, no balloon, no centerpiece, no snack that I attempted to help with that didn't first come with a "How are you doing?" inquiry from the person in charge of that segment of prom setup. Sometimes I answered honestly – that I wasn't OK at all. And sometimes, I responded with a somewhat casual, "Well, you know, I'm as good as I'm going to be right now," because I simply did not feel like rehashing the event as many times as people were asking me to.

Not long after my arrival, the students began to line up outside, awaiting their requisite breathalyzer test to enter the prom. As I expected them to, Kevin's group of friends showed up before most other students. They had spent the day grieving together, making shirts to wear over their dresses and tuxes in Kevin's memory. Kevin's best friend, Caleb, organized the shirt production, and as the prom began, he was permitted to announce that anyone who would like to purchase one from him could do that.

I made my way through the evening the best I could – as the night wore on, I grew weary, exhausted emotionally as much as I was physically by the events of the day. Arriving home that night allowed me my first opportunity since that morning when the news of the accident started flooding in to really reflect and think about how I felt.

I climbed into bed, finally feeling the weight of all that happened over the last three days, and my body responded by melting into my covers, welcoming the sleep that invited itself to take over my heavy eyelids.

As I drifted off, I returned to the questions I started with: How did this happen? Did this happen by chance? Was Kevin looking for a way out of the hole he had dug for himself by wrapping himself up unnecessarily in the affairs of the grownups around him? I had no answers to these questions, only a pit in my stomach that told me everything I needed to know about what happened.

What I didn't know at the time, was that it would be years before I was able to acknowledge what was true, rationalize it in my mind, and put it in a place in my brain and in my heart where I could live with it.

After all, how does a person walk through her life with a knowledge like this and be OK?

It would be a long time before I would be able to live with what I knew – and processing that this was only the beginning had not yet even started.

9
Chapter

The Funeral

Until Kevin's accident, I lived in a happy place where death was for old people, and teenagers got to be kids and not worry about losing their friends. Until Kevin's accident, the thought that my students would ever die literally never crossed my mind. And until Kevin's accident, I thought teaching was going to be mostly about books and writing – I didn't consider that death would be a part of my job – but losing Kevin taught me that death is for the entire human race, including myself.

The mortality check I experienced following Kevin's death was sobering and fast. It was unrelenting, and at my age – I was so young, only 23 – contemplating the idea that I would someday cease to exist wasn't something I allowed to cross my mind much, and the relatively small age difference between Kevin and me dragged all of those uncomfortable thoughts right to the forefront of my mind. Considering the fallible nature of my own existence wasn't something I was used to. But in the days following the news of Kevin's death, I found myself in this place – and frequently unable to remove myself, even to engage in basic daily functions, such as going to school and doing my job.

The first important hurdle I had to clear following Kevin's death was attending his viewing and his funeral. From what I knew about Kevin's injuries caused by the accident, it was hard for me to fathom that there would even be a showing, but there was.

The death of a loved one is an interesting time in the human experience. It tends to bring people together who otherwise may not have been, and, unfortunately, it also has the ability to tear people apart. In my case, Kevin's death brought me the best friend I never had, and never thought I needed.

Kaitlyn was Kevin's counselor. She was the faculty member aside from myself with whom Kevin was the closest, and she had been the initiator of many investigations and conversations related to Kevin that year. She was the person at school that spoke to Kevin last, and she was the one who called his mom and begged her not to let Kevin out of her sight. If anyone tried the hardest to save Kevin, it was definitely Kaitlyn.

She called me in my classroom on the day of the showing.

"Hey, I'm leaving for the funeral home about three today. Wanna ride with me?" she asked.

Relief washed over me, because I really didn't want to do this on my own. "Yes, oh my gosh, please," I said.

I didn't know this at the time, but I am so glad life gives you who you need when you need them. God's gift of Kaitlyn in that moment and on that day was an incredible expression of the timing and wisdom of a higher power.

Kaitlyn and I went to Kevin's showing together, and for the next eight or nine years after that, we never stopped doing things together. Now we live in different states, and life has gotten complicated, but we still talk frequently. I still love her more than I could ever say in words, and I know that on the day of Kevin's viewing, in April of 2007, I was meant to hop into the passenger seat of her car.

And so I did.

As we drove to the showing and Kaitlyn and I made small talk, trying to ease each other's anxiety, I felt the pit in my stomach grow. Was I strong enough to see him like this? What would his mom and dad say to me? Would they know or understand the secret truth that the rest of us knew and understood – and if they did, would they say it out loud? How would I interact with the parents of someone I knew had died in this way?

We arrived at the funeral home at the same time as some other school officials and faculty members. As we walked in, I clutched my purse and crossed my arms around it, trying to ward off the shiver that threatened to travel through my body. It was the end of April, the weather was warming up, and yet I was freezing, shaking a little – squeezing my purse against my trembling body seemed to somehow offer me some safety. I held on, hoping it would give me the strength I needed to face my grieving students, to talk to Kevin's mom and dad, and to somehow, in the midst of all of that, process and handle my own emotions.

As we entered the building, we were met by several students and fellow faculty members – the line to give our condolences to Kevin's family was long, and as we waited, we watched several students file out, crying and holding each other, looking for comfort.

One student, Danna, who was also in my English 12 class with Kevin, seemed to find comfort in no one. Our eyes met, and as she walked over to me, tears streaming down her face, she practically fell into my arms, heaving sobs onto my shoulders as I held onto her and assured her that everything was going to be OK. In my ear, she whispered, "How could he do this? How could this happen?" as she cried and cried.

Though I did not – and still do not – know the answer to this, a teacher's role is often about comfort and support more than it is about anything else. So that's what I gave her. I just held on and let her cry as long as she needed to. I let her ask the hard questions to which none of us had the answers, and I offered a silent prayer that this would be the last time in her life she would ever have to feel this way.

Thirteen years later, through social media, Danna and I still chat and stay in contact, and many times, on the anniversary of Kevin's death, she will message me to see how I am doing. In one of those messages, on the tenth anniversary of his death, she said, "You were the first and only person who just held me and let me cry. Thank you."

It's important, I think, as a teacher, and as a human, to just hold people and let them cry sometimes. I didn't do anything special for Danna that day. I didn't impart any wisdom to her; I didn't explain the "why" behind Kevin's untimely death. I wasn't able to bring him back or to ease her pain. But I was able to be there. And I think sometimes, just being there is the most important part of the grieving process.

The tough part about the being there when you're a teacher, is that there is rarely someone who can be there in the same way for you as you handle your own grief.

Luckily, I had Kaitlyn, and over the years we processed so many of our own feelings together, but teachers often are faced with grief, sadness, overwhelm, and anger to deal with all on their own. Who holds the teachers and lets them cry? Who hugs them until they don't need it any longer? Who tells these teachers that everything is going to be OK? The answer is often no one, which leaves teachers feeling both isolated and worn out. You see, I didn't know it at the time, but death was something I was going to face over and over again in my career – just in the first seven years of my career, I would lose six students. And at no point in the loss of any of those young people, did anyone other than Kaitlyn ask if I was OK.

*** *** ***

The line to give our condolences to Kevin's parents wrapped around and through the funeral home. Kaitlyn and I stood in this line together for over an hour – maybe even two – waiting to express our sorrow to Kevin's mom and dad. Danna wasn't the only student I hugged or greeted during this time – there were many, and in between shared expressions of grief, I only wrapped my cardigan tighter and held my purse closer to my body in an attempt to gain some of the comfort I so desperately needed myself.

It never came.

When we finally reached the point where it was time to greet and console Kevin's parents, I remember shaking as hard as I ever have in my life. A race of thoughts: How do I comfort them? What do I say? Do they know how this happened? How are they even breathing?

I still don't know the answer to most of these questions, but I do know that when I saw Kevin's mom, her eyes lit up with recognition. She reached for my hand, led me over to Kevin's dad, and said, "This is Lindsey. She's his favorite teacher."

At which point, the tears came. And they didn't stop.

It was like in that moment, I received permission to accept that Kevin was dead, that he was lying there in front of me, in a casket, flanked by his parents, and all the tears and shivering that had been held inside my body – behind my purse and inside my cardigan – came rushing forth at once.

"I am so sorry for your loss," I remember saying, quietly and through my tears.

His mom's strength in that moment amazed me then, and still does today. "Thank you for loving my boy," she said to me.

I cried harder. And then she hugged me – she didn't let go for several seconds.

All the anger and frustration and lack of understanding of the "why" behind Kevin's death vanished in that moment. In 2007, I could not articulate why this happened. But in 2019, as someone's mother myself – I know exactly where it went. All of it – anger, uncertainty, fear – all of it ran together in that moment as human compassion for this mother who was no longer a mother to any living children. And I cried. I cried for my pain and hers. I cried for a lost role that this woman would never fill again. I cried for the death of a young soul who, no matter how tormented, was lost too soon.

The truth was that I DID love Kevin. He made me

laugh, he made me smile, he frustrated me, and he showed me human compassion – or what I thought was human compassion – in the single-most difficult year of my life.

Had he betrayed me? Yes.

Had he lied to me? Yes.

Had he done the unthinkable and endangered others to further his own agenda? Yes.

And yet, the emotion I felt for this child was then, and is still today, love.

You see, teachers love their students even when their students make bad choices. Teachers love their students even when they act like kids and do kid things – and at the time, I thought Kevin just had done a bunch of those kid things all at once. So, with the limited information that was available to me in that moment, I was also incapable of understanding the depth of what I was dealing with – and without that information, what I felt for him was love, and what I felt for his mom was the sincerest sorrow that I'd ever experienced.

So, Kevin's mom thanked me for loving her son. And I accepted her thanks.

Then, Kevin's mom did something that I will never forget.

She took me by the hand and said, "Come here. There's something I want you to see."

I allowed myself to be led by her, and we walked around the front of the casket, where Kevin's head rested peacefully on a pillow. And as long as I live, I don't know that I will ever hear more heartbreaking words than the ones she said to me then.

"Here, come with me. If you stand here, and look over

him from this angle, it sort of looks like him."

We stood over the edge of the casket together – she held my hand in one of hers, and with the other, she ran her fingers through her dead son's hair. She was right – the damage that had been done to Kevin's body from the accident made it difficult to identify familiar facial features, so we stood from a different angle, trying to find Kevin on the face of this stranger lying before us.

Again, I shivered. Kevin's mom squeezed my hand even harder.

I didn't see Kevin on that face lying in that casket. Nowhere did I see the carefree kid that I had met not even one year before. And nowhere did I see the malevolence that I felt like I needed to see in order to believe what people were telling me had really happened just a few short days before.

And then just like that, it was over. I released my hold on Kevin's mom – again expressed my sorrow and my grief, received her expressions of gratitude, and Kaitlyn and I moved on our way so the next group of mourners could offer their own sentiments to Kevin's family.

*** *** ***

The following day, it must have been Tuesday or Wednesday of that week, we attended Kevin's funeral – several of us from school were able to have our classes covered so we could leave school early for the service. It was held at the funeral home we'd visited the previous afternoon. The service was nice – nothing too out of the ordinary, and it paid as much tribute to Kevin as was possible – his uncle delivered the eulogy, and its focus was on his daring spirit, his zest for life, and his ability to make almost anyone laugh.

I knew these traits existed in Kevin, and as I sat there, having my hand held by my principal, I allowed the heart-break of the duality of this young person's humanity both fascinate me and bring me to tears. This time, I let them fall.

As I rode home in Kaitlyn's car for the second time in as many days, I allowed my mind to wander – to Kevin, to the accident, to the two other kids who had survived, one barely, this terrible tragedy. My thoughts swirled – inter-twined with my grief were feelings of betrayal, feelings of uncertainty, concerns about what this all meant moving forward, and just how I was going to process losing Kevin knowing what I knew – after all, just days before, I had been called into an office where I was told that my life was potentially in danger. Just days before, I learned of a conver-sation in which Kevin informed Kaitlyn that she would not see him the following school day. And just days before, I had driven home with a sigh of relief that nothing "weird" had happened at school on April 20.

I blurted out what I was thinking to Kaitlyn. "Do you think he did this on purpose?"

"Oh my God," she said. "Yes."

I remember sucking in my breath, reeling a little from what she said, and realizing that the pit in my stomach was coming from a real place. That I wasn't off-base when I was feeling sick. That the feeling that something was just "off" about this situation wasn't exclusive to me.

*** *** ***

Kaitlyn and I talked for a long time that day after we

got back to school. We went around and around the accident, and the days leading up to and immediately following.

And after that, we never really stopped talking.

Death is a funny thing. It doesn't discriminate; it doesn't stop for anyone. It just takes from the living, sometimes without reason or explanation, and then those left behind are supposed to make sense of the taking. Kaitlyn and I were not meant to make sense of death on that day, but what we were meant to do was begin a friendship that now spans two decades, and that, since Kevin's passing, has included weddings, divorces, other funerals, blood, sweat, tears, therapy, friends, and the birth of my son.

I didn't know when I lost Kevin that I would be gaining this type of friend, but I do believe the universe brings us who we need when we need them, and certainly Kaitlyn and I needed each other in this time, and for the several years that followed.

*** *** ***

Summer came just in time that year – about five weeks after Kevin's death. The warm weather invited comfort for me for the first time in many months. I was still grieving Kevin's death – nothing prepares a person for what the traumas of teaching will bring – but something about the sunshine allowed me to finally sit down and take a deep breath. I didn't know at the time that this would be the case, but that summer, and for the thirteen summers since then that I have been a teacher, I have allowed the warm weather to bring me comfort, solitude. I have allowed myself to soak up the time off as a break from the emotional taxation that drains my mental and physical reserves every school year. After one year of teaching, I had no idea how tired I really was – but I found the rest to be so welcome and so, so good.

Kaitlyn and I spent that summer largely together, reading by the pool and resting our weary hearts in preparation for the next batch of students that would be charged to our care the following August.

On one of our pool days, Kaitlyn brought me the most precious gift a person can give a bibliophile such as myself: a book recommendation. She had heard great things about a book called *"We Need to Talk About Kevin."* So we thought we'd try it.

The book was about a teenager named Kevin – the irony of this was not lost on me, nor was it lost on Kaitlyn. In the story, the fictional Kevin was a mentally ill, loner of a teenager, who had engineered an act of mass violence at his school. The book is told from the perspective of the character's mother, who is trying to explain her feelings about her son and the times and ways that she concealed actions of Kevin's that seemed suspect or strange – all actions that could have been precursors to an act of school violence. All actions that she and her husband had ignored. All actions that lead to one truth: Kevin was a sociopath. The book is told through letters to her husband, as she visits her mentally ill, criminal son, in prison. Needless to say, it's a heavy book.

As Kaitlyn and I read it, we processed and talked through our feelings and reactions to our real-life Kevin's death. The book was probably not something we should have been reading so soon after Kevin's death; for some reason, though, we kept going. Maybe it's because neither of us believes in not finishing a book that we start. Maybe it's because we're glutton for punishment. Maybe it's because we were so shaken by his death that our own judgment was impaired beyond what we were capable of understanding.

I didn't know the answers to why we kept reading at the time, and I doubt that I could put a finger on it now, but I know that we should have stopped. I know that it wasn't healthy for us to read about something so close to home. I know that there were so many events from the book that were so similar to our lives that previous school year.

And yet we kept going.

And as we kept going, we brought ourselves around to the truth – the truth about what had happened leading up to the accident, and the truth about the feeling that maybe Kevin was going to do something "weird."

After so many hours of going over and through those events, and after so many days of reading the same book, we arrived at the real truth of the matter – we needed to talk about Kevin.

10

Chapter

The Truth

 F ive weeks after Kevin's death, on the last Friday night in May of 2007, I sat in a folding chair on the high school's gym floor, watching my seniors file in, dressed in their caps and gowns, as the sounds of *"Pomp and Circumstance,"* played by the band, floated through the air.

Graduation signified so much that year – an end and a beginning – to so many things: the completion of a first school year as a teacher, a health scare in my own family, the beginning of my friendship with Kaitlyn, and the establishment of myself as a professional for the first time. As the notes to the song were punctuated, one by one, I was able to take perhaps my first deep breath in ten months and to reflect on the events of that year – the good and the bad – as I held my head high with the pride of accomplishment: I had made it.

I had survived my first year of teaching. And the weight of the concept of survival was not lost on me as I looked back on a year full of challenges and heartbreak. Was there joy? Laughter? Happiness?

Absolutely.

But the prevailing emotions that year had been fear,

sadness, and uncertainty.

And even though I had spent much of that year afraid, sad, and unsure, I still held my head high. As I watched my students file past, I allowed the tears welling in my eyes to stain my cheeks.

The graduation ceremony began as most do – introductions of faculty members, school board members, and notable members of the community. As the focus of the ceremony shifted to the graduates, and as Kevin's mom and dad were introduced to accept a diploma in his memory, my thoughts floated back to that day, just five weeks before, when our principal called us to the office to talk about Kevin, and said, "We think he's going to do something weird."

I didn't realize at the time that this would be the catalyst for the single most career-and-life-shaping event that I had experienced to date. Even thirteen years later, I still believe that Kevin's death is the most significant contributing factor to both who I am as a teacher today, and to who I am not.

*** *** ***

As I watched the ceremony unfold, tears continued to fall intermittently, and my thoughts drifted back to the events leading up to and immediately following Kevin's accident. Having Kaitlyn to talk to in the weeks that followed turned out to be such a blessing – I had a place where I could go to share my innermost thoughts and fears – and she mostly agreed with them. I had a person who knew Kevin as well as I did, if not better, and I could freely say what I was thinking and feeling without fear of judgement. So many of our conversations circled back to one question: had Kevin done this on purpose?

That one question led us to so many more. Had he taken his own life? Why had there been other people in the car with him? Were they aware of what he had planned? Why would he make a decision like this?

But none of our questions came with answers, because the person we needed to ask was dead. The other two students who had been in the accident weren't able to be much help. One was critically injured in the hospital, and the other one, though virtually unscathed, was difficult to reach – not only did she speak cryptically about the accident, school officials didn't place much interest in her take on the events leading up to the crash. But, over time, we did get a pretty good idea of the situation's reality by talking to this young lady. Her injuries had been minimal, and her memory of the events leading up to that fateful Friday night had been stronger than any of us were expecting. Those memories, we found, were also somewhat disturbing.

Over a period of time that isn't specific to me because revealing these details was not a responsibility with which I was charged, we learned that school officials hadn't been too far off as it related to Kevin's plans. While he may not have opened fire in a school building, Kevin was bent on destruction of some kind, and as his plans for that Friday were thwarted, he moved toward what Kaitlyn has referred to as a "suicide pact" involving Missy, the young lady who survived the crash.

What we also learned in that period of time was that notes between Kevin and Missy were exchanged outlining their plan.

There is no easy answer to this question of why a third young person was in the car, as there has never been any indication that Casey had any awareness at all of what Kevin and Missy had planned.

Thus, the disturbing pieces of the puzzle.

*** *** ***

What we knew was this: In April of 2007, Kevin was suicidal, and he was just enough of a showman to want to make this public knowledge by committing an act of mass violence in a school building. We knew, also, that notes and letters, and probably text messages, had been exchanged between Kevin and Missy, plotting – were they plotting their own deaths or those of hundreds of other high school students? That, we will never know. Somewhere in this exchange, these two young people agreed to end their own lives, and to do it together.

What we didn't know then and still do not know is how Casey ended up in that car.

After years of piecing this together, it appears that Casey merely got into the back seat that night. No logic exists other than this – Casey was not suicidal. He had plans to be a Marine – his graduation was not in jeopardy; he had friends who loved him; he seemed to know what his present looked like and to be content with what his future would hold.

The only literal explanation for Casey's presence that night was coincidence. So, he, unknowingly, got into a car with two of his friends, presumably to go to the gas station for a snack, not knowing that this one decision would change the course of his life forever.

*** *** ***

The truth of this situation is a heavy one. It is inconceivable to think that a teenager, let alone two, would want to die – and yet I know this is the case way more frequently than it should be in this world. It is heavy to think that a teenager who wants to die would be willing to carry out a plan like this, collecting collateral damage like Casey and Missy, along the way. It's even heavier to think that this same teenager could have considered mass destruction in the form of human lives – Kaitlyn and me included – by committing a violent act inside a school building on purpose.

Thankfully, Kevin's plan for school violence never came to fruition. In that way, school officials were lucky, and they were prepared as well as they could have been. But his suicide pact was unstoppable, and for that, I have carried a certain amount of guilt over these years, and I know that other school officials have felt what I have felt. Could we have done more? Could what we did do have been done differently? Could Kevin's life have been spared? I don't know those answers because the God of the Universe who loves and protects people and calls them home when it is their time only reveals to us certain pieces of His plan at a time.

Reading this now, I wonder if there were ways that the situation could have been different – handled differently, played out differently, all of that.

But know this: the people in my life who handled what Kevin was about to do at the time did their level best. These administrators, not so different from you or me, had never been faced with a potential act of school violence on this scale before. These teachers, myself included, had never taught a student like Kevin before – and hopefully never will again. So, when you're reading this, please remember that. Please keep in mind that 2020 is a different world than was 2007. Unfortunately, several more acts of school violence all around the country have taught us how to respond appropriately and quickly to threats like the one we felt Kevin posed – but time and experience were not on our side back then. And truly, I'm thankful for that. The lives that have been lost and shaped by school violence this past decade break my heart – and I am so beyond grateful that we did not become a statistic that day.

The unstoppable part of his plan – his pact with Missy – was something none of us could have predicted. While we knew that he was suicidal, we couldn't have imagined that he would have taken another young person, let alone potentially two – with him. Nothing our school officials could have done would have prevented his making this decision – I know that now, but at the time, I was so racked with guilt over my power to stop it, that I could barely function.

*** *** ***

Some people will read this and think I've completely lost my mind. Some people will read this and believe this surely isn't true. That there is no way a situation like this could have unfolded in a small, peaceful Indiana town like mine.

There are some people who, to this day, believe that what happened with Kevin and his friends was all a horrible accident. They believe that the coincidences of those two days in April, 2007, were the stars aligning in just the right set of accidental circumstances for almost everything to go wrong.

I am not one of those people.

For me, the truth exists in a different way, and it always will.

For me, the truth of the situation was this: Kevin was a very, very sick young man. He had a mental illness that went undiagnosed and – to my knowledge – untreated. This mental illness led him to feel less than his worth, and to therefore contemplate and carry out his own death. I believe that Kevin killed himself that day because he didn't see another way through his own fears and insecurities. I believe that he latched on to Missy because she, too, was somewhat troubled in her youth.

But I will never know why Casey got into that car.

I will never understand the mental illness that drove Kevin to take his own life that fateful night.

Part of me wonders if Kevin felt that his acts of deception related to events at school like the disappearance of my keys and the phone tree and maybe some other areas of his life just felt too big, and so he saw no other way out. I truly hope that this is not the case, but I can't help but wonder.

Part of me wonders if he came to my neighborhood that night and grabbed Casey because he needed me to have a visual reminder of that accident every day for the rest of my life. I believe that he was sick enough to think this way. And for a long time, I did have a daily reminder. I drove by the crash site for four years after Kevin died. And every time I passed it, I said a little prayer for Kevin, and wondered in the back of my mind if this was some kind of statement that he was making to me on that night. After all, I had distanced myself from him at the direction of my administration, but also for my own good. I had essentially turned my back on him and refused to really re-engage in a relationship with him, and for a person like I believe Kevin was, this would not have been received well. He never said anything like this to me – but in my soul, I know.

*** *** ***

Some parts of what happened in those two fateful April days will never make sense to me. And they definitely didn't make sense to me while I watched my first graduation ceremony as a teacher on that Friday night at the end of May, 2007, either.

For thirteen years, much of my life has been shaped by what happened – or by what didn't happen that day, that it's hard to really sift through a "before" in terms of myself as a person.

What I can tell you is that Kevin's death marked an end for me. Losing Kevin was the end of the person I was for the first 23 years of my life, and the beginning of the person I became. What I didn't know at the time, was that it would take a very long time for me to come to terms with, and to love, the person that the circumstances of my life had forced me to become.

As the graduation ceremony came to a close, my students filed out of the gym that night, finally turning the page on their high school careers. What I didn't understand at that time was that even though it was now officially over, it would be a long time before I was able to turn the page on my first year of teaching.

Chapter

The Next Four Years

The tree that marks the location of Kevin's last moments has been gone for 13 years, replaced by an extension of the homeowner's driveway, paved over shortly after his accident. To the naked eye, or to someone who wasn't looking, the new pavement doesn't look any different from the old. But to me, the person who drove by it every day for over four years after his death, I know right where it starts and stops. I know right where the tree used to be, and what it used to look like. I know how driving past that driveway made me feel nauseous for years. I know the feelings of guilt and helplessness that came with seeing that patch of pavement going in and that tree coming down.

I know, because I know the truth.

*** *** ***

As it often does after someone passes away, life went on. I started year two as a teacher, full of fresh hope, having rested and done little-to-no school-related work for ten weeks. Kaitlyn and I spent the summer by the pool, reading, talking, processing, and working through, to the best of our abilities, some really complicated feelings of guilt, shame, hopelessness, and fear. We were sad, too, sure. But the amount of time we were able to dedicate to the sad was small in comparison to what we needed to process in terms of our other complex emotional reactions to what had happened to Kevin. We truly didn't have much time to be sad.

We read our book – "We Need to Talk about Kevin" – which, as I mentioned before, was a mistake. Not in the sense that the book was bad – no, not that. But in the sense that neither Kaitlyn nor I were in a place mentally where we could process or handle our feelings about an incident so similar to the one we had just lived through.

We floated through that summer, soaking up as much Vitamin D as we could, working out together, and generally spending as much time as possible becoming best friends. An unintended consequence of losing Kevin was gaining Kaitlyn, and for the seasons of my life that she has walked through with me since then, I am grateful. I know that the universe always intended for KJ and I to have each other; I just didn't know what we would have to go through to find each other.

During that second teaching year, my mom got better – and then she got sick again. Cancer seemed relentless; it would not leave us alone. After another major surgery and radiation treatment, her health improved, the cancer was gone once again, and life returned to somewhat normal.

Earlier that spring, before Kevin's death, I had agreed to marry my first husband. And because of what happened with Kevin, I don't know that I focused much on our engagement until school was out for the summer. Scott and I finally figured out a date for our wedding – the following spring break – and we married just shy of a year after Kevin's passing. I remember thinking of Kevin on my wedding day – would he have known? Would he have been there?

I know now that I would probably have never agreed to marry Scott, or to follow through with this marriage, had my mom not gotten sick, and I do believe that Kevin's death was a contributing factor in my mental state as well. As time passed in our engagement, red flags presented themselves that I simply ignored. As someone who doesn't drink alcohol often, being engaged to a person who drinks between eight and ten beers a night can be unnerving. And as much as I tried to talk myself out of being worried about that, I allowed it to continue, and I allowed myself to accept that it was part of my life now. So I married him – and shortly after we got married, I learned that drinking was the least of my concerns.

Scott was older than I am – not by a ton, but enough that he wanted to try to have babies right away. I agreed, and the process of "trying" began. I never thought that I didn't want to have children, and at the age of 25, I did feel mature enough to give it a shot. Looking back, that makes me laugh, but at the time, it seemed reasonable. In the time that we tried to have a baby, we never once achieved a successful pregnancy, and so some medical testing began. If you know anything about infertility, it is a roller-coaster of emotions and a loss of dignity through all of these crazy personal medical tests that remove all of the love and passion from having a baby. As the test results started to roll in, some more red flags appeared. Sure, my body was being crazy, not performing the proper tasks in order for a pregnancy to occur, but Scott's was, too. We found out that there were some issues on his side as well, and through that revelation, I began to discover that my husband had a serious problem: he was addicted to prescription medication. Several months went by, and the situation escalated past the point of repair. After just shy of three years of marriage, Scott and I divorced, adding still another traumatic event or series of events to what had already occurred in my short teaching career.

*** *** ***

I worked at my school for seven years, learning how to be a teacher. In those seven years, I lost Kevin; I nearly lost my mom, and a grand total of six of my students died.

After a particularly difficult student loss – about three months after Kevin – I stormed into the guidance office, looking for the director, Jenny.

I barged into her office – I didn't even look to see if she was busy. Luckily, mid-rant, I realized she was alone: "You're going to have to give me some coping skills to deal with this. Or I have to quit," I remember saying to her.

Jenny's reply haunts me to this day: "There are no coping skills. You just get better at it," she said.

Her words were scarily accurate. There's nothing quite like the feeling of numbness you get when you've experienced student death as much as I have. It never stops being hard. It never stops being horrific. It never stops breaking your heart. But at a certain point, there is a numbness that washes over your body and never really leaves you. At a certain point, it stops shocking you – and that's when you know you have a problem.

My problem? I got too "good" at losing kids. The autopilot responses that I still have today have never truly left me – get the phone call, go to school and hug kids, read the statement from the administration out loud in class, and allow kids as much space to grieve as they need, while offering an ear to listen and a hug and a Kleenex when the inevitable tears begin to flow.

Lather, rinse, repeat.

How had this become my life?

How does a teacher lose the ability to feel anything when a child DIES?

How does a teacher know exactly what to do and spring into action without thinking or processing any of her own feelings?

And – for that matter – who hugs the teachers when these kids die?

The answer? No one.

*** *** ***

I remember my breaking point well.

Looking back, the inevitability of a breaking point is laughably obvious, but at the time, sustained by my youth and by my ability to pull in and virtually ignore all of the problems in my life, I carried on, consciously unaware of the crash that was headed my way.

Four years had come and gone, and by the end of that fourth year, I had just acquired an apartment for myself post-divorce. I had recently finished graduate school. And while Kevin's loss wasn't at the forefront of my mind anymore, it was still always there – still today, I am not the person I was prior to what happened in that first year with Kevin, and I never will be again.

I know now that the transformation of my heart was the result of something called compounding trauma – the idea that consecutive traumatic events can occur was foreign to me until a therapist told me that this is what I was experiencing. I lost Kevin. I nearly lost my mom. I lost my marriage. I had a colleague attempt to take advantage of me. I lost my home. I eventually – not for two more years after my divorce – left the first teaching job I'd ever taken because it was the best decision for the life that I was creating to replace my old one.

I also learned during this time that if a long-term response to a trauma exists – beyond a few months – it's unlikely to ever go away.

Much like the pavement on the driveway where Kevin's tree once stood, my heart was resurfaced after we lost him. It was transformed permanently, and what existed there before April 20, 2007, will never exist in that space or in that way again.

Each loss, each death, represented a layer of asphalt on my heart, one that was roughed up and paved over again with some roughshod method of healing that I chose at the time – usually those methods involved a treadmill and chocolate cake, so as you can imagine, no complete acceptance of myself as a new person, as a trauma survivor, took place for quite a long time.

One night, after a particularly intense treadmill run at the gym, I did my usual: I took my shower, I put on my pajamas, and I got into my bed to read.

And as I attempted to settle into my book – and was unable to do so – I realized that something was wrong.

Very wrong.

12

Chapter

Trish

Four years after Kevin's death, I found myself in an unusual place. I was still teaching, but my first husband and I were in the midst of a divorce, and I moved into a new apartment with a high school friend who was in a similar situation to mine. My mom had been healthy for a few years, I had just finished graduate school, and even though I'd been through several tough moments during my divorce, including losing 28 pounds that I did not need to lose, I thought I was fine. I thought I had coped with all of what life had thrown at me, and done so fairly well.

I thought that I was functioning at a pretty high level, but it soon became apparent that I was wrong.

I have never been a night owl – staying up late is tough for me – and it doesn't take but about two days of being off my sleep schedule for me to feel pretty off-kilter. So one night, just after I settled into my new apartment, I climbed into my bed a little after 8 p.m. – even now, if I could do this every night, I absolutely would. I picked up a book from my nightstand, likely one from the *Game of Thrones* series, and opened it to read. About three page-turns later, I realized that I hadn't absorbed a single word of what was written on those pages. My mind wasn't racing. In fact, for potentially the first time in my life, I found that it was literally doing nothing. I went back to the beginning of where I had started to read, and I tried again, but with no luck. My eyes were passing over the words on the pages, but none of the content was being absorbed. My hands were turning the pages of the book, but out of routine rather than necessity.

Not only am I an early-riser, I'm also a lifelong bibliophile, and my love of books has seen me through some of my darkest days. But on this day, I could not force my brain to concentrate on what was happening in the book. It was the first time this happened – but it absolutely wasn't the last. Night after night, this went on for weeks. I would pick up the book with the intention of reading and then, before I knew it, I would be staring at the wall, mindlessly turning pages, or not moving at all.

This inability to focus stretched into other areas of my life as well. I would get into the car, set out to drive somewhere, and space out for the entire drive. More than once, I arrived at my mom's house – after 30 minutes of driving – with no recollection of how I had traveled there at all. The drive was nonexistent in my memory. The scary part was that this spacing out, this apparent dismissal of reality, happened every day for several weeks. I wasn't getting lost in my thoughts as I drove to work or to see family; I was not having any thoughts at all. I even remember my mom asking me several different times what I wanted for dinner, where I wanted to go, what I wanted to do – and every time, I'd just tell her I didn't care. Because I legitimately did not care about *anything*. I found myself staring into space, not concentrating on anything, and not feeling anything, either.

My dad always told me I had a really "busy brain," so this newfound fog was not something I was accustomed to, nor something I liked all that much. Thinking and feeling nothing was completely new, and I was not on board. I never knew there existed in humans the capacity to feel nothing. I never knew that in these same humans dwelled the possibility for numbness so deep, so core-cutting, and so raw that it could literally rob a person of the ability to feel anything at all.

For the rest of my life, I will be fascinated by the concept of nothingness – because I have felt it. I will be fascinated by nothingness because I have tasted it in tears streaming down my face, uninvited, unprovoked, and surely unexpected. Almost daily, it seemed, during this time, I would find myself crying – seemingly out of nowhere. It was a strange phenomenon, this nothingness – it came to me, also, as I stared through people and things, and not at them, realizing too late that the images I was supposed to be processing or remembering were gone.

I will now forever be fascinated by nothingness, because this nothingness has the power to be everything. It has the power to consume a person – to swallow her whole before she's even aware that she, too, has disappeared into nothing. I will always be fascinated by the paradox that is nothing, and yet is everything.

The sort of all-consuming nature of what was happening to me was unnerving, but it was my lack of ability to understand it that scared me the most.

I didn't know it was possible for something like this to happen, and it wasn't until several years later that I realized that trauma response is a real thing. It wasn't until quite some time, even after THAT, that I was willing to admit I was, in fact, a trauma survivor.

Even now, the weight of those words is such that they are difficult for me to say. It sounds trite to me, almost silly. I didn't die. I didn't even ALMOST die. I just could have. Tons of people have parents who survive late-stage cancer. The divorce rate in this country is off the charts. As far as I know, there was no ACTUAL gun at school on the day I was in danger. So, what did I have to be sad about?

*** *** ***

I think one of the best signals of growth in a person's life is when he or she is able to recognize when something is too big, or too much. The phrase "God won't give you more than you can handle" really bothers me, because I think the point is that God gives you more than you can handle all the time, and THAT is how you grow. I think that is the beginning of evolution, the beginning of self-love and acceptance. After several months of being a stick-thin space cadet, I finally came to the realization that maybe I wasn't doing as well as I thought I was, and that maybe the anxiety medication my doctor had given me wasn't quite enough to bridge all the gaps I had in my life at that time. After all, sustaining oneself on a steady diet of German chocolate cake and six-mile speed runs on the treadmill just wasn't cutting it, either.

In the teaching profession, I have found that I have not just made friends with my colleagues, but instead I have expanded my family. Teachers really get each other – we have similar lives, similar interests, and similar struggles.

And we DO LIFE together. As a teacher, it's really hard to remember to be a human being and to feel real emotions, because teachers are "on stage" in 50-minute life increments for ten months of the year.

Our colleagues become our safe place of connection – and it was a connection like this one that led me to Trish.

Trish was a therapist, and she was recommended to me by a teaching colleague who is also a great friend. She handed me Trish's card as I passed by her classroom one day, no doubt in a hurry to get somewhere else – teacher speed is unlike any other professional speed. In a hurry with no time to stop and chat, I simply grabbed the card, huffed out a "thank you" and kept moving. Trish's card sat on the corner of my desk at school for several days before I had the nerve to call to make an appointment, but when I finally was seated in the waiting room at Trish's office, there was no doubt I had done the right thing.

I will never forget the first time I saw her. Trish was a tall woman, probably close to six feet. She was slender, had chin-length dark hair, and a beautiful olive complexion that I envied so much. She had kind eyes – they were deep, dark brown like her hair, and they shined when she talked. She barreled around the corner in her office building, maxi skirt swishing behind her, and cheesing at me from ear-to-ear with her hand outstretched to shake mine. Shyly, I shook her hand and mumbled some sort of awkward greeting. And then I froze. I'd never been to a therapist before. What the heck was I supposed to do now? Go pour my heart out to a complete stranger? How was I supposed to even pour out the contents of something that felt so empty?

She guided me back to her office, and when we got

there, I refused to sit on the couch. I told her I would prefer not to because sitting on the couch was "too much like therapy."

Her response was perfect: "You're aware that this is therapy, yes?"

Still, I refused the couch. In fact, for the two years I was under her care, I never once sat on that couch. I made her do it, and I'm sure she wrote down my aversion to couches – and to therapy – in her copious note-taking.

The first question she asked me was, "Why are you here?" I couldn't answer her. I remember just staring at her like she was supposed to know the answer. Like somehow she would have a sixth sense that would tell her what was wrong with me so I wouldn't have to.

Because I felt nothing and everything simultaneously, it was too difficult for me to really articulate what I was doing there, so I just said, "I think I'm really sad."

And we went from there.

*** *** ***

She told me we could start with sad, that sad was a good place for beginners. And, oh, what a beginner I was.

She smiled at me, and we talked about sadness. She smiled at me, and we talked about happiness. She smiled at me, and we talked about loss. And with every smile, we dove a little deeper and went to work. We worked for what seemed like forever at filling the void that the nothingness had created inside me. What did we fill it with, you ask? We filled it back up with me. The pieces of myself that I thought were gone forever? We invited them to come back. Where we needed to create new pieces to fit the new puzzle of the person I had become? We did that, too.

After a while, the nothingness didn't feel so empty anymore. It didn't feel like it owned me, and was therefore everything. In our sessions, we made lists. We planned activities, and we took spiritual journeys together. We laughed, we cried, we swore, we yelled.

And we figured out something very important: that what I thought was one hard year – the year of my divorce – was really five hard years. And that the five hard years started with my mom's cancer diagnosis and with Kevin.

I learned that those five hard years also included a new career and the loss of several students, not just Kevin. We concluded that his death was obviously the most traumatic, but that compounding traumas and triggers also were present. Five hard years included a fellow male colleague who I thought wanted to mentor me and be my friend, but who really wanted to see how far I would allow him to take our relationship, even though we both were married at the time. These years also included a colleague who was so blinded with hatred and jealousy that her mission for one calendar year was to see to it that my teaching contract not be renewed. And, we concluded, my divorce was just the icing on the proverbial cake.

As we worked through these "significant life events," Trish gave me a variety of coping skills that I could use to master the parts of my own personality that I could control should they arise again. She took great pleasure in assigning me homework that, little by little, helped me fill in the void that had once been created by the idea of simply "Being Sad."

She loved assigning me "homework." I learned from

her that she saw several teachers, and that she was always giving her teachers different assignments. These tasks were work we would do at home before our next session together. These things started small, things like call your mom and tell her you love her; delete that creepy colleague's number from your phone; eat a real meal, not just chocolate cake.

Little things added up to big things, and they were all geared toward the business of letting go, of releasing control. I am aware that holding on can sometimes make a person stronger, but I learned from Trish that holding on to things that really matter and holding on for the sake of control are totally different. Why could I only eat chocolate cake? Because I could control the chocolate cake. Ten bites? OK. Five bites? Also fine. What if I want to eat the whole pan in one sitting with a fork? OK, go for it – because I can.

"What if you just ordered a cheeseburger in a drive-thru on your way home tonight?" she asked me.

"A cheeseburger sounds disgusting," was my reply.

"That's your homework, then. Order a cheeseburger. And eat it. Every last bite. And then tell me how it went when I see you next week."

Ever the people-pleaser, I followed instructions. I ordered a cheeseburger from the nearest drive-thru on my way home: light ketchup, no onion, extra pickle. I tried to eat it, I really did. I took a few bites before the nausea set in. As I choked down the rest of the burger, I sat in my car and sobbed. What had happened to me? What had made me like this?

The answer was control. I had felt and been so out of control in so many other situations in my life, that the smallest thing – food – was an area where I felt I could regain some of what I had lost.

I never threw up that cheeseburger. I could have and I wanted to. Instead, this was the first successful digestion of many cheeseburgers to come, so we ruled this homework assignment a success.

*** *** ***

Perhaps the most important homework Trish ever gave me, though, was the day she told me that my homework was throwing rocks.

"What?" I said.

"Yes. You're going to throw rocks. Do you know anyone who has a pond?"

"I do..." I said softly. At this point, I was still relatively confused.

"OK. Call that person and see if you can borrow their pond. You're gonna throw rocks into it."

"Why?" I asked.

This came after a particularly intense session in which I admitted that I was very angry about what had happened to Kevin. I was angry about my inability to stop it. I was angry about my own role in it. I was angry that HE was so angry and sad that he wanted to die. I was angry that I didn't realize this was happening. I think I was even angry about being angry. As anger is apparently a stage in the grieving process, Trish chose this moment as a teachable one.

"You are so mad, and we can't go any further with healing until we let some of that go. I don't know how you're going to let it go without some sort of physical release. So you need some rocks."

127

The summation of my homework assignment was this: Fill a bucket with rocks, and purchase a helium-filled yellow balloon. Grab a pair of scissors – we'll get to those in a minute – and take said rocks and balloon to the borrowed dock, sit on that dock, and throw those rocks into the water until they were gone.

This was definitely the strangest homework assignment I had ever been given, much less planned to execute. I almost bailed on the whole affair, but then the people-pleaser in my personality resurfaced. I was reminded that I really don't like to disappoint people, and so I set out to complete my homework. How interesting it is to me now that completing this assignment was more about not disappointing Trish than it was about my own healing. It turns out, though, that this was a total head-fake expertly executed by Trish to trick me into letting go of some of what I had been hanging onto for so long.

On the day of the rock-throwing, I followed Trish's instructions to the letter and set off to complete my assignment. In truth, I thought it would be easy. All I had to do was sit on a dock and throw these things into the water. Then I could leave, right? Wrong. What I learned that day was that there is so much more to rock-throwing than I ever knew – and that this day was meant to be a major turning point in my journey back to myself.

I situated myself on the dock, barefoot, legs dangling over the front edge. The bucket of rocks, the scissors, and the balloon sat to my right. For a moment, I sat there and took in the peaceful scenery of the pond. A duck or two swam by, fish made bubbling noises, and I may have even swatted a mosquito. Then I picked up my first rock. I tossed it into the pond rather carelessly, still unsure why I was doing this. Then I picked up another one and threw it, a little further and with a little more force this time.

A third, a fourth, and a fifth rock flew into the pond – and then the image of Kevin's face appeared as the first tear made its way down my cheek.

The rest of the time that it took to throw the rocks passed in a blur, and by the end, I was sobbing, my hair had fallen almost completely out of its ponytail, my clothes were filthy, my makeup was running, and snot was streaming out of my nose. Yeah, glamorous, I know. When the last rock plopped into the water and the bucket spilled over, I looked out across the pond, and I remember yelling "Why?" at the top of my lungs several times before I realized that not understanding – not ever understanding – was OK, was normal, and was part of being among the living after the loss of another human life.

In my fury, I completely forgot the yellow balloon. But as I settled down, wiped my tears, and took my place back at the end of the dock, the wind blew it into my peripheral vision, and I remembered what had to come next. For so many years, I held on to my anger, to my sadness over Kevin's death. His loss, compounded by so many other significant, negative life events, had been my cross to bear for such a long time, that I had never even considered the business of letting it go.

There are events in our lives that mark significant "before" and "after" moments, and this, for sure, was one of them. I had never taken the time to picture the "after," or what it might look or feel like. Kevin's death – and the events leading up to and immediately following it – felt so pervasive for so long that the idea of allowing myself to move forward without carrying this heaviness everywhere I went never even crossed my mind.

I remembered Trish's final instruction: "When you're done throwing all those rocks, I want you to pick up the scissors and cut the string. The balloon will fly away, and in that moment, I want you to let it go. I want you to feel your life starting again, and embrace that. I want you to allow a new beginning to happen."

So, I did.

As I watched the balloon float upward, further and further until it was just a speck and then nothing at all, I felt a lightness in my heart that I had not felt for many years. I felt my body exhale in a way that said, "It's over now. You've done all you could do. And you're going to be OK."

And I was OK.

I was able to resume my life almost immediately after that. I started eating all the cheeseburgers my stomach could hold. I started reading again, and I could comprehend what I read. I cared about who I was talking to and what they were saying. I even met the man who is now my husband, and was able to begin and maintain a healthy relationship that wasn't laced with grief and guilt about things I couldn't control.

*** *** ***

In the months that followed the rock-throwing episode, Trish and I were able to cut our sessions back from once a week to once every other week, and eventually to once a month. I can't say that I didn't miss seeing her every week, but I was so thankful to have my life back, that I was more excited to see her and tell her about all the amazing things that were happening, that it really didn't matter. Because of Trish, the nothingness that I couldn't describe when I met her was gone. Because of her, I had the courage to live a life that I could never have imagined for myself, and because of her, I understood that there are things about me that some people might consider weird, odd, or even bad.

But I also know because of her, that these things are just part of me.

I am positive now – and I will be positive for the rest of my life – that she saved me. I will always be indebted to her for the time she gave me, for the compassion she showed to me, and for the pieces of myself that she revealed to me. Because of her, I am alive. She took me on journeys to the deepest parts of myself – some that were dark, ugly, and scary – and she revealed to me a person that I really kind of like.

Therapy is like finding a really good girlfriend and being able to confide in her all the secrets in your heart. I am so thankful to her for being this girlfriend in my life, and for making me feel safe confiding in her all those secrets of my heart. I am most thankful, I think, to her for keeping those things safe, for holding sacred the things we shared, and for knowing just what I needed and when.

In the middle of our time together – or what I thought was the middle – I lost Trish. She, as she put it, had just "a little bit of breast cancer." I think it was more than any of us realized, possibly even Trish herself, and she died somewhat suddenly on Easter Sunday about seven years ago. I received repeated phone calls from her office on that following

Monday morning, but since I was at school, I thought they were just aggressively confirming my Wednesday evening appointment. I didn't even call back until the evening, and when I did, as I was driving home from work, her secretary shared the news that she had passed away.

I remember my mind going dark for a moment, nearly inviting back in the nothingness that had brought Trish and I together in the first place. But I heard her tell me no. Losing Trish felt like losing a best friend – the pain was sharp, it cut deep, and it hung on for a long time. But in my grief, I was able to hold on to the sound of not only her voice, but of her telling me that it was OK to feel pain, but that it was not OK to unpack and live there. "Feel it. Feel it completely," she would say, "and then release yourself from it, learn what you're supposed to learn, and move on."

I've learned so many lessons since Kevin's death, but perhaps the most important of these lessons has been the ability to feel and to express gratitude. I was destroyed by Kevin's death. I was destroyed by Trish's death. But destruction is not all there is. Because of them, my life will forever hold a place for gratitude. And each time I reflect on the things in my life that I am grateful for, I will remember Trish.

I will remember her because she pulled me out of the nothingness and reminded me that there are things in life for which I need to be grateful, and that a full life begins with gratitude. I will remember her because she asked me why I was there, and that question had such a deeper, more meaningful answer than anything I could have come up with at that time.

I am so grateful that she showed me why I am here –

not just in her office on that chair, but here, alive, on earth. That gift is precious and rare, and for it, I have eternal gratitude.

13

Chapter

Teacher Trauma

Growing up, I think we, at many different stages, believe we are who we are always going to be – like, "This is it. This is me. I know who I am and I'm not going to change anymore." When we reach milestones in life – having babies, turning a certain age, getting married, whatever it may be – maybe it's at those milestones that we think we're finished changing. Maybe at those points in life we stop and think that nothing could shake who we have become because we have finished the business of becoming.

I'll never believe that age 23 I thought I had finished becoming who I was going to be in my life, and I don't think I've even neared the finish now – I sure hope not, anyway. But I will say that the shock or the fascination with just how much can change in a relatively short period of time will never stop perplexing me, driving me forward, inspiring me to be better – frankly, to invite more change.

What a paradox this life is in that way.

As those years pass and change, so do we. I remember when I had my son, my mom told me one of the wisest things she's ever said: "You'll just go in and out of the phases with him, and it will feel natural to you because you won't know any different."

She was so right. But the interesting part of this wisdom – from my VERY smart mom – is that it also applies to so many other areas of life. I had no idea the phases of my life that my teaching career would encompass. I could never have predicted that within eight months of starting my life as an adult professional that I would face and survive a trauma that would shape almost every other area of my life, and that it would fundamentally change who I had been as a person when that year started.

It took me a long time – years, in fact – to be able to speak out loud that I was the victim of a trauma. But the uniqueness of my trauma was that I was the victim of something that never happened. I survived being unsafe in a school for one day of my life – I didn't get shot –I don't think I even almost got shot. I don't even know for one hundred percent sure if that was the plan. I didn't get in the car that night with Kevin and alter the course of my life forever like Casey and Missy did – but my trauma has always been, and will always be, in the unknown.

What would have happened if he had brought a gun or a knife to school? What would have happened if the extra security was necessary that day? What would have happened if Kevin's parents, or Casey's parents or Missy's parents hadn't allowed them to leave their homes that Friday night in April of 2007? What would have been different about their lives?

What would have been different about my life?

Heck, I don't know. And I never will. And that, my friends, is the trauma. The unknown. The what-ifs. The wondering.

I have wondered, and I have worried, and I have replayed the events surrounding Kevin's death a million times. I have wondered if there was something more I could have done to save him. I have worried that I somehow caused his death in some way. And I have gone over and over the events in my mind until they just start to spin out of control, no longer making sense.

Wondering can really do something to a person – it's like an earworm – like a song that won't leave your head. It plays over and over and over again until you can hardly stand it anymore. And the questions never stop coming.

The questions are why I went to Trish. The questions are why I went to our Guidance Director and asked her to help me. The questions are why I nearly walked out of my high school that May evening after that first graduation and never, ever went back.

*** *** ***

Trauma is a "psychological emotional response to something that is emotionally stressing or disturbing," according to the Center for Treatment of Anxiety and Mood Disorders. For so long, I had trouble saying the word "trauma," and I didn't know where I fell on the spectrum of those feelings and experiences, but I knew that I for sure felt distressed and disturbed by Kevin's death and by the questions I asked myself afterward.

Understanding that I am a trauma survivor is something that has taken me years. It is something that I struggled with admitting, with understanding, and with acknowledging. After all, like I've said before – I didn't die. And I don't even think

I almost died. But I DID suffer a "psychological emotional response to something that was emotionally disturbing." I know now that Kevin's accident was only the beginning, the catalyst for my trauma. I know now that his accident, my mom's cancer, my divorce, and my run-in with a colleague who struggled with appropriateness all contributed to my eventual emotional bankruptcy.

But at the time, I just thought I was sad.

At the time, I just thought that not eating was something that was happening because I legitimately didn't feel well – I did nothing to investigate the root of my not feeling well; instead I just carried on with it as it became a part of me, and I made no effort to change it. I added six strenuous workouts a week to not eating much of anything besides German chocolate cake, and I ran myself silly on a treadmill for nearly an hour each and every day.

Looking back, it had to have been because I thought if I just kept running, I would eventually get somewhere inside my head. But an unhealthy mind is itself like a treadmill – it gets a person nowhere, and the only place my unhealthy mind was able to land me was in therapy.

*** *** ***

And thank goodness for that.

Therapy gave me a reason. Therapy taught me to feel things, and not to run from them. Therapy taught me that my trauma responses – taking things to extremes, irritability, shortness, sharpness of the tongue – were normal, were warranted. Therapy taught me that instead of running from my feelings, I had to walk through them. I had to feel them.

And that feeling them was OK. The only thing that was not OK, Trish told me, was unpacking in my sadness and living there. And that's precisely what I had been doing.

Not long after my divorce process began, I scheduled myself an appointment with my family doctor. It was at this appointment that I was prescribed my first dose of anti-anxiety medication. Apparently, my jittery mannerisms, my general irritability, and my intense apathy for most aspects of life were not normal.

When I said before that Trish saved me, I mean it. I felt such shame for taking this medication – unfortunately the shame was not all self-inflicted. Even family members judged me for taking the medicine, encouraged me not to "rely" on it, and told me that my anxiety wasn't real.

But do you know what Trish told me?

She schooled me on trauma. It was from her that I learned that I had, in fact, suffered a trauma, but it was also from her that I learned one of the most common responses to trauma is anxiety, followed closely by irritability.

Do you know what happens to me when I'm having a panic attack?

You guessed it. I become ridiculously irate; I snap at people; I am short with people; I have a sharp tongue. And for a long time, my awareness of these responses caused me to believe that sometimes I'm just a jerk.

Wrong.

I'm snippy, short, and sharp when I am anxious.

I am anxious because trauma made me this way.

Is that wrong?

No.

Is it just who I am?

Also, no.

Anxiety is not who I am, and it never will be. But anxiety exists in my life as part of my after. Anxiety exists in my life because I have been unsafe, insecure, and afraid in nearly every aspect of my life–and the lack of security happened all at the same time. But it wasn't until I talked to Trish and began the healing process that I was able to understand that. She also taught me that if a long-term response to a trauma exists – past a few months – it is unlikely that that particular response will ever go away.

Sure, I'm less anxious at different times in my life. I have triggers that are all over the place – but I know them now. I anticipate them much more effectively than I used to, and not only am I able to harness my thoughts much more quickly than I was able to do so in the past, but I am also extremely open and honest with people. I'll simply say, "Look, my anxiety is off the charts today – I'm not sure why, but we are all humans here, and I could use a little compassion."

I even do this with my own students because I am a believer in the connections among human beings. I am a believer that humans need to hear about others' humanness, in all its raw, messy, uncomfortable glory. Because that is when really beautiful relationships are built, when incredible trust is fostered, and when, just for a minute, those walls we put up between ourselves and the world come down and we are able to look at each other and say, "Yeah. Me, too."

One of the things I've found that I think it's hard for others to understand sometimes, is that the clear before and after that exist in my life are not going away. The person I was before my first year of teaching and all that came with it is gone forever. I am irrevocably changed by those events.

Are all of those changes good? That's a tricky question, and truly depends on what you think of as "good." I think a better question might be, "Are all those changes allowing you to become the best version of yourself that you can be?"

I think the answer to that question is yes.

The older I get, the more acutely aware of my own mental health I become.

I think not only are those changes allowing me to know and love myself better as a human, but I think, perhaps more importantly, that the changes have taught me to be a teacher I never would have been able to be if they hadn't occurred. They have taught me to be a person in front of a classroom, and not just a talking head. They have taught me to encourage students in their own vulnerability in a judgment-free zone. They have taught me that without this vulnerability, the experience in the classroom is far less authentic, and something I don't want to be part of as much as I do when the walls come down and the trust goes up.

*** *** ***

Teaching is one of those professions – you know the ones – where people are either amazed that you're able to do it, or they're sort of apathetic to it – and sometimes they even ask me questions like, "Why do you subject yourself to something like that?" Or they make snide comments like, "You're so smart. Why don't you do something where you can use your brain?" And to those questions, I usually just laugh. There's a statistic somewhere that relates the number of decisions a teacher makes on a daily basis, and the number is staggering. I think it's into the thousands – of decisions – every day. So, when someone asks me something like that, I usually smile to myself, because if teaching isn't a good use of my brain, I really don't know what is.

Once, I was at some group event, talking with some friends. There were people there who were new to the crew, who didn't know that both my husband and I are both in education. Those people are always my favorite. They always have the most to say. I was having a glass of wine, chatting, laughing – you know, the usual. And a new acquaintance walked up and joined our conversation. As it usually does, the conversation turned to what we all do for a living. This new acquaintance had so many questions: How do you DO that job? Aren't kids these days INSANE? What about phones? How do you handle those? Don't you ever just want to smack them? Aren't kids so disrespectful?

And you know? Sometimes kids are insane. Sometimes their phones make ME the insane one. And yes – sometimes they are SO disrespectful.

But do you know that I have never taken those aspects of my job into account when I have considered whether or not to continue in this career? That's right. Not once. I have literally never thought to myself, "One more disrespectful kid, and I'm out."

Not. One. Time.

I'll tell you what I HAVE considered, though. And it has nothing to do with kids. It has nothing to do with books or writing or grading so many essays I can barely see or anything remotely even like that.

What I have considered, many times over the years, as I have taught and coped with trauma after trauma and the loss of way too many young lives – and with learning to love myself as a teacher and as a human in the mess that comes after these heartbreaks – is the question that literally no one has ever asked me:

Are you OK?

*** *** ***

I don't think anyone outside of education – naturally – would consider what might happen when a student passes away. I don't think anyone outside of education also can comprehend the daily lessons that teachers impart to children that have nothing to do with the lesson she planned for the day. And when the lesson that the kids need help with is "Why did this happen?" these grieving students need to have the answer.

In my career, I have literally spent countless hours sitting with kids, talking or in silence, who have grieved the loss of a young life that we have in common. I have literally spent countless sleepless nights mulling over how I will ever explain that even though we think death is only for old people, this is not always the case. And I have literally spent days of my life in therapy, coping with what is left of me when I am done giving parts of myself away to students who are consumed with grief, often processing the first death they've ever faced in their lives.

And in those countless hours, when I am counselor, mom, shoulder-to-cry-on, tissue-supplier, advice-giver, listening ear, and everything in between, somewhere in there, I lose my own humanity every time. And I never know quite how that happens. Somewhere in between hugging everyone else's children, I lose my own feelings. I push them down, out, and away from myself, because I don't have time to focus on them. I've probably given as many as 50 hugs in a single day after the loss of a student. I've driven from my apartment 30 minutes away back to school at 11 p.m. on the night of a student suicide for the sole purpose of hugging other people's babies.

And you know what?

Even if I would trade it for anything – and I wouldn't – except getting those lost young people back – I still sometimes wonder how teachers manage the mental load of something like this. I wonder how I have managed it so many times myself.

And in all of that management and navigation of "hard stuff," no one has ever – EVER – come to me and said, "Hey, I know you're struggling because you knew this kid too. Are you OK?"

That has never happened.

And you know what else?

That's simultaneously OK and not OK, and the contradictory nature of this part of my job just makes sense to me because it is my world. It is what I do. And it is how I have felt my way through the last fourteen years, somewhat blindly at times, trying to figure out how to do this job and to do it well. This has required a profound understanding that things can be OK and not OK at the same time – that accepting this contradiction is part of the deal, but that the contradiction can also wear a person out, can cause a person to really wonder if this job called teaching can really be done at all.

When I feel the fatigue, and when I feel the burnout,

and when I wonder if I can emotionally stand to do this job for even one more year, I know that there are others who are feeling it too. I know that there are others who are walking into school, feeling so drained they can barely muster the strength, and I know that I am not alone. When I am feeling this way, whether it is after a student death, or even just when the week has been particularly heartbreaking or hard for other reasons, I always wonder one thing: who is going to hug the teachers?

Who is going to tell the teachers that everything is going to be OK?

Who is going to tell the teachers that time will heal their wounds?

Who is going to reassure the grownups that death is only supposed to be for old people and that this – this tragedy, this unspeakable truth that sucks your soul and breaks your heart – is someday going to feel OK again?

You see, if you're not a teacher, you probably don't know that most teachers put themselves last in literally every situation. It could be something as small as foregoing a restroom break to answer a kid's question or to have a conversation during a passing period. Or, it could be something much bigger, like being the person someone else's child needs when there is a tragedy or a crisis.

I've worn all those hats over the years, and it never gets easier to make myself a priority when other people are hurting. It never gets easier to reclaim my own mental health when the dust settles after an event like the death of a student. It never gets easier for me, and so I know that it never gets easier for the rest of my colleagues all over the country and the world. The only "easier" thing is being aware of what I need, knowing that it's going to take some time, and giving myself the grace to do that – but friends, that didn't happen overnight. It's been an ugly, mind-numbing, infuriating, process of growth–at times fueled only by pure grit and stubbornness that I will not allow this to be the thing that breaks me, or that takes me away from the career I've worked my entire life to establish.

*** *** ***

There has to be someone who hugs the teachers.

There has to be someone who tells the teachers that everything is going to be OK.

There has to be someone who reassures these adults that even if it doesn't feel OK right now, that it will again someday.

Teachers face traumas every day – their own, and the traumas that are brought into their classrooms by the students they teach. And navigating the business of educating students who have suffered in the ways that many of our students have suffered is no easy task. Doing this while, at times, simultaneously experiencing traumas of our own, is next to impossible.

You see, trauma survivors live and love differently. And so do teachers. There is no separation from trauma, and there is no separation from the love and care that we have for these young people.

So, when someone asks me if I have ever considered leaving teaching and doing something else, of course the answer is that yes, I have. I think about it almost every year. And it's NEVER because I'm sick of essays or literature or teenagers. It's NEVER – well, OK, not never, but darn close – because teachers aren't paid the way they should be. It's NEVER because I don't like my job or my students or my colleagues.

No, none of those things are factors in my decision to remain a teacher.

The singular factor that has ever swayed – or nearly swayed – my decision about my career is this one: who is going to be there for teachers? Who is showing up for us while we are showing up for everyone else?

All too often, the answer has been no one.

Not because the people aren't there, but because no one knows what to do or say.

But in the face of all of this – the uncertainty, the heartbreak of humans at every level in education – my challenge and my call to action is this: we must take care of our teachers. We must hug them, literally and figuratively, so they feel safety and love and so they feel the security they need to feel to do their jobs and to do them well–so they continue to give. But we must give back to them. We must make sure that they are not only willing – but that they are able to continue walking through the phases of their lives as teachers. We must lift them up; we must support them, and we must protect their humanity   so they can protect our children.

Chapter

My Son's First Lockdown Drill

On August 4, 2019, I sent my only baby to preschool. That morning, I woke him up, I picked out his clothes, I packed his lunch, and I loaded him in the car to take him to a place I'd never left him before. A school. A real school. With teachers and classmates and curriculum.

That morning, I gifted him a little bracelet with a silver star charm an orange cord – I'd bought these for both of us to wear that day, explaining to him that when I looked at mine, I would think of him, and that if he missed me, he could look at his and think of me too. As this morning fell only two days after my son's fourth birthday, it was not without intense emotion that I sent him off, backpack almost as big as he was, lunchbox in hand, to conquer the wide world of preschool.

My son has been in the care of another adult since he was eight weeks old – an adult by whom we were so blessed. She took care of my baby as if he was her own. She was me when I couldn't be me so many times – the gratitude we have for Andrew's first daycare provider is unmatched. But there was something so grown up about this idea of pre-school, and a class, and a teacher that had the mom in me reeling. It took way longer for me to adjust to preschool than it did Andrew.

Within a week of his starting school, we were juggling show and tell schedules, snack calendars, lunch boxes, supply lists, enough art projects to wallpaper the entire house, newsletters, new friends, and–intruder drills.

Intruder drills?

Yes. Those. The ones where your kids hide and pretend they're playing a game to be as quiet as they can. The ones where they're really practicing making themselves as small as they possibly can in case a lunatic with a gun barges into a preschool and tries to hurt innocent babies.

Cue the urge to vomit.

You know the one.

You especially know it if you're someone's mother.

It's even worse if you're also a teacher.

Ever since I found out my son's school has procedures in place for an event like this, I've been simultaneously thankful and disgusted. That this is the world we live in really bothers me. That this is the world I will help my son navigate scares me. That this is what he will someday ask me about, with fear – and maybe even with tears – in his eyes, literally eviscerates me. Schools are supposed to be safe havens – places where children can go to learn and to grow and to flourish – not to hide from some mentally ill socio-path with a gun who is bent on destruction and inflicting pain onto others.

That thought makes me physically ill.

And it's only intensified as Andrew has gotten closer to

going to Kindergarten.

When he does start Kindergarten, in the fall of 2021, he will be exactly one mile away from the school in which I currently work. And I will hate that. One mile seems so close – but it's so far away if he's in danger and I can't get to him.

He will know what to do because he will have practiced hiding. He will know what to do because his teacher will take care of him. He will know what to do because he's a smart boy and a good listener. But there's nothing he can do if a crazed gunman opens fire inside his school or his classroom if procedures aren't implemented properly or if teachers aren't willing to do whatever it takes to protect him.

And you know what?

Something about that really bothers me. Because someday, as a teacher, the shoe could be on the other foot.

What if it's my building? What if it's my classroom? What if it's my students?

More vomit.

Because here's the absolute truth: I do NOT know how to manage being a mom and a teacher in a situation like that. I do not know how to step in between a gunman and my students, knowing that I could be the one who dies that day – and then it's my son who grows up without his mom. I really just do not know.

Being a mom changes everything about who a woman is – the mom part of me didn't exist before my son was born, so in a way, I, too, was born on August 2, 2015, when he entered the world. I am lucky in this life to get to experience motherhood in a way that many women don't: not only am I mommy to Andrew, but I have the most incredible, beautiful bonus son, Jack, who entered my life in 2011 – he prepared my heart to be Andrew's mom, and there isn't a day of my life or Jack's that I won't be grateful for what he taught me about being a mom before I was one.

But since August 2, 2015, nothing has been the same, and I would trade absolutely none of it. It's interesting to live in this dichotomy of absolutely loving my job and absolutely loving my sons, and also knowing that someday I may have to choose who to protect and how to protect them. There are days when I look at Andrew – or Jack – and my heart absolutely breaks at the thought of the state of our world – how could this be the place where they will grow up? How do I tell them that someone might want to hurt them someday, and yet still reassure them that I will do everything I can to protect them?

And then there are days that I am so ANGRY that I even have to think about choosing between someone else's child and my own. First-year teacher Lindsey would never have thought twice. She would have thrown herself in front of a bullet for her students; she would have hidden them from any and all violence and danger that might have presented itself. She would have died for them.

Mother-of-two Lindsey? Not so much.

This version of me knows that it is my job to protect my students, but this version of me also knows that my children – Andrew especially, and only because Jack has a great mom –deserve their mom. They deserve to grow up in a family that is in-tact, and part of my job as a parent is to ensure to the best of my ability that this happens for them. Can I control my own destiny? Absolutely not. But the anger

I feel and the bile that rises in my throat when I consider a world in which I don't watch my babies grow up is something that intensifies with every news report of a school shooting. It's something that grows every time we have a lockdown drill at school or every time I hear that the pre-school has practiced theirs yet again, always without letting on to these innocent babies that they are not simply playing hide-and-seek.

And I bet I'm not the only teacher mom who has felt this exact emotion at one time or another.

So, what do I do? How do I continue to function in this role as teacher and mom and not lose my mind or worry myself to death?

*** *** ***

When my son is in Kindergarten, I'll be a mile away from him, and if a lunatic with a gun enters his school, there will be nothing I will be able to do to stop that. In that way, I'm no different than every mom in the United States who is at work or who is at home, trusting a school to keep her kids safe. I'm no different than any other teacher who has children in the school system where she works, again trusting that school to do its job and to return her babies to her at the end of the day in the exact same condition in which the school received them that morning.

We are all the same in that way.

I just sometimes wish the weight of that responsibility wasn't so significant.

I just sometimes wish it was within the fibers of who I am to be able to say that I won't take drastic heroic measures to

153

help other people's kids if it means not being able to go home to my own kids.

But here's the truth: I know that I will. I can talk a big game and say that my own kids will win – and to the best of my ability, I will make sure that's true. But you know what? Those thirty faces I'll be standing in front of, those thirty students who will be looking at me for what to do next? They're someone's babies, too. And it's not within my being to not make sure, to the best of my ability, that those babies are also returned to their mothers in the same conditions in which they were entrusted to me that morning.

I just sometimes wish the weight of that responsibility wasn't so significant.

But it sort of answers all of our questions, doesn't it?

It's the fibers we've woven through this book.

It's the idea that I am a schoolteacher, and that I am someone's mother, and that I have promised to protect so many children. I have promised to care for the ones who live in my home, and the ones who don't. I have promised to lock doors, shush teenagers, and teach them how to be as small and as quiet as they can be – just like those preschool teachers who are teaching my son to play hide-and-seek.

So aren't we all in this together? Aren't we all doing the exact same thing day in and day out?

Aren't we all just showing up for these people, hoping, praying, and expecting, that someone is going to show up for us and our kids should they be placed in a situation like that?

You see, this obligation is a circular one, and it encompasses us all.

I just sometimes wish the weight of that responsibility wasn't so significant.

*** *** ***

I don't think that, until I was Andrew's mother and Jack's step-mother, this thought played much of a role in how I coped with what didn't happen with Kevin at school that April day in 2007. Like I said before, it never even occurred to me that maybe I should stay home from school that day – but trust me, it occurs to me now. It occurs to me all of the time. And you better believe that, should I ever find myself in a situation like that again, I won't step foot in a school building until that threat is vanquished. But there's something else you have to remember: we didn't know any better.

None of us did – no one knew how to handle a threat like the one we thought Kevin was making that day. It wasn't a bridge we had crossed before, and thankfully not one we have crossed since. I'm so grateful for what the administration at my high school did to protect us that day – because they did everything they knew to do and were capable of doing. They took the actions they took because it's what they deemed necessary at the time, with the knowledge and training and information that they had. And I'm so grateful they took this potential threat seriously.

Can you imagine what would have happened if they hadn't? Can you imagine the potential for danger and tragedy on a day like that? I don't even want to think about it, and so, I don't. For the most part.

Or, I didn't. Until I was Andrew's mommy.

Until I was his mom, I didn't think about what it meant to protect other people's children not knowing if I will get home to my own.

And that, I think, is the essence of where I'm coming from.

In this vow to protect our students, are we not all risking our own lives and our own families? Are teachers not again committing to show up for everyone else before they show up for themselves? Aren't these educators again demonstrating their selfless natures, their dedication to the youth of this nation, and their absolute commitment to safety at all costs? Regardless of the credibility of the threat, or the level of potential violence of the threat?

And yet.

Who is helping these professionals process what they have vowed to do? Who is supporting these teachers' mental health, their spiritual growth, and their overall OK-ness as they make these commitments and sacrifices day in and day out?

*** *** ***

Someday, both of my sons will read my book, and they will have questions for me. Kevin's story will disturb and scare them, as it disturbed and scared me all those years ago. Someday, my boys will process the idea that there was a day in the timeline of my life that nearly caused our family to never exist.

They will ask their questions.

And do you know what I will say to them?

I will tell them that in their lives, they will face hard

things. That hard things are a part of life, and that our job is to keep going, to keep fighting, and to keep healing. I will tell them that going through hard things is a guarantee, and that feeling pain is OK. But what is not OK is unpacking in their pain and living there. That they must walk through the hurt to get to the other side of healing, to move forward with their lives.

And if they look at me with tears or with fear in their eyes with questions about school, I will remind them that I will do my best to keep them safe, that I will trust their teachers to do the same, and that they, too, must have faith in the process, because this is truly all we can do.

If my sons want to know about Kevin, I will always say his name. Because speaking his name, even in death, means that he lived and was real, even if he was sick. Even if he needed help that he never got. Even if he scared me – more than I have ever been scared before, and even if he broke my heart more than my heart has ever been broken before – he was a real person. He was a human being, and when his mom looked into his eyes, she saw in her son what I see in my son: pure, unconditional love for this little human whom she created and who depended on her for his survival.

My heart will always break for Kevin's parents – they will never experience some aspects of this life that they thought or hoped that they would – and so, I will always say Kevin's name. And I will never say it with hate or disdain – only with the understanding that this was a young man who was very ill. That this was a young man who struggled profoundly with this existence on earth, and who paid the ultimate price for his struggle.

But when I talk about Kevin, I won't focus on the day

we weren't sure what he was going to do. I won't focus on feeling unsafe. I won't focus on his death, or the uncertainty that I felt about what he was doing for all those months that first year of my teaching career or why he was doing it.

No, that's not what I'll share with my sons.

I'll focus on the lessons, on what I gained. I'll focus on what this experience has taught me about humanity, about vulnerability, and about allowing people to see who we really are. I will focus on asking for help when we need it, about human suffering, and about healing.

And I'll focus on teaching them that there are times in our lives that we must show up for other people, no matter the cost.

Chapter

Teacher Trauma: It's a Real Thing

How we approach teacher trauma as a society going forward will define and shape our teachers' career experiences more than ever before. As this story is being told, our world is in the throes of the COVID-19 pandemic, and for a large part of the recent past, we have been confined to our homes in order to slow the spread of this deadly virus.

But what does that have to do with trauma? Plenty, I would argue. I would argue that now, at the hands of a virus we don't know a ton about, we have all – every school employee, student, parent, etc. – been a trauma victim.

How?

In a matter of weeks, life as we knew it came to a screeching halt. Our grocery stores were suddenly overrun with hoarders; our news outlets crammed with stories about the death and destruction the virus was causing around the world; people were asked to stay home to slow the spread of the virus; schools closed their doors with a quarter of the school year left; businesses ordered non-essential employees to work from home.

And at the time that this is being written, we largely remain there — home.

When teachers go back to school, if it's this fall, this winter, or next spring, we will go back to a school that doesn't look much like the one we left. And what we are returning to remains to be seen. Will we have to wear masks? Will we be required in some way to monitor social distancing? How will we do that?

In a matter of months, the world has been turned on its head. I've never been more personally or professionally uncertain in my life. I've been back to school to get supplies a few times, and until recently, the date of the last school day I taught in person was still on my board. It looked like a rapture happened: students' belongings still scattered on desks, forgotten pens and pencils, stray water bottles, papers containing the names of students who will never step foot in my classroom again.

If that's not traumatic, I don't know what is. When we go back, we will all be processing our feelings differently than we did before. We will all be processing new feelings, ones we've not experienced prior to now.

And more than ever, we will need our schools and communities to step up, to step in, and to support our emotional needs like they never have before.

Here are some things we can do:

1. What Schools Do to Keep Us Safe

Maya Angelou once said, "When you know better, do better." Fourteen years ago, when I began my first year in the classroom, the frequency at which mass acts of violence occurred was significantly less than it is now. I don't think we need to just focus on schools to agree that our world has become somewhat desensitized to these heinous actions, and that we see reports of them in the news all too often. I've been clear that I didn't know – that none of us knew – what Kevin was truly planning on that day.

The administrators at my old high school did their absolute best. They had incomplete information, speculations and hunches that drove their decision-making on that Thursday in April of 2007. And they did what they could with what they had.

I have said before that it literally never even occurred to me to stay home that day. Maybe it should have. It would today. But none of that reflects in ANY WAY on the efforts that were made by the administration to keep us as safe as they could. Again, they did what they could with the information they had. And I felt safe.

I never once thought that I was not their priority that day or that they didn't take the threat seriously or that they weren't doing absolutely everything in their power to keep everyone in that building as safe as possible.

School safety measures have changed a great deal in a decade and a half. The school where I work now has a concrete plan for intruders, which we practice several times a year. We have different types of drills and procedures to match the possible scenarios that could arise. And we train our staff to execute them with precision.

If we didn't have this at my old school fourteen years ago, it was NOT negligence. It was merely a reflection of where we were in the continuum of school safety evolution at that time. If we did have these procedures, I don't much remember them – or we didn't practice them at the frequency we do today.

What's tough is the reality, right? The reality that no matter how rock solid our plan – no matter what building or school corporation or state or community – we are all susceptible to an act of school violence at any given time. Statistics show the communities where school violence is most prevalent, and it's not in the ones you might think. In fact, places like my first school – and like Brownsburg, where I currently teach – are places that are similar in demographics to the ones where tragedies have occurred in the past.

We must be aware of incidents like the one that occurred at Parkland in South Florida – where they had a plan – where they trained to execute the plan – and where that very plan failed at every level.

Just like at Parkland, it is everyone's goal to keep every single school safe, every single day. History has shown that it is impossible to do that. But if there are failures, we must examine the how and the why of those failures so we can do better for our own communities if a situation like that should ever present itself.

Now, we know better. We know that we must prac-tice and execute these procedures, and that we must have the tough conversations that scare us and make us uncom-fortable and we must learn that these conversations open doors to keeping us safe. After all, we are not ostriches; we cannot bury our heads in the sand and pretend this isn't real.

We know that every administrator takes these threats seriously; we know that it's their goal to ensure that everything runs smoothly in the process of training teachers to respond in crisis situations. It was like that at my school thirteen years ago, and it's even more so now – in every school – and because as the world has changed, so have the threats.

We know our teachers are on the front lines when our students are in jeopardy. We know that they are the ones hiding in rooms, praying no one enters or tries to enter with the intention of hurting schoolchildren. We know that they are expected to take drastic measures if necessary in order to keep those children safe – but if we know this, AND we are armed with the knowledge that these teachers also know exactly what to do, we are already in a better situation than we were in fourteen years ago.

We know better, so we must do better. And it is my belief that teachers, when placed in situations that challenge them, will always do that.

2. Relationship Building

The core of our success as educators will always be in the relationships we build with our students.

Human beings are hard-wired to need connections with others. We live in a society that, at every turn, removes those connections. Heck, I never have to leave my house if I don't want to – I have Amazon Prime.

One of my favorite authors, shame researcher Brené Brown, shares her thoughts on human connection in her body of work on vulnerability and shame. It resonates with me, as I think it is one of the most applicable bodies of research that can be practiced in a classroom. She says, in

"The Gifts of Imperfection," that "Authenticity is a collection of choices that we have to make every day. It's about the choice to show up and be real. The choice to be honest. The choice to let our true selves be seen."

We need to allow our students to really see us. We need to be more than talking heads at the front of a room.

If we do this, they will allow us to see them, cultivating a judgment-free environment in which we can all thrive, grow, and become who we are meant to become.

These relationships are the cornerstone of our success as educators.

And yet we have to be OK with building the relationships knowing the hurt involved. Vulnerability is never free, and even when it hurts, it's always worth it.

I don't know a single student who has ever felt connected in his or her school environment who has committed an act of violence against the adults and fellow teenagers in his or her life. Not one.

3. Focus on Mental Health

Counselors must be able to talk to students on a regular basis. And these conversations should not always be about college or testing or the student's pathway to graduation.

I think most people feel like since they've been to school, they know how schools function, and they also have opinions on how they think schools should function.

This does not exclude our legislators, who think regulating public schools and school teachers at every level and at every turn is the answer to reforming education or holding schools accountable for student success.

What that means is the amount of time that teachers and counselors can spend actually talking to kids and building relationships and fostering connections with them is drastically reduced.

What that also means is that the place where students should feel the safest and most connected besides their own homes is a place where they, in many cases, don't look up.

And why would they?

In their minds, no one cares about them. In their minds, they don't have to interact with real humans because they can make all of their friends on the Internet and in their games.

And what are schools doing to stop that? Nothing. Because they can't. There is no time. The time these school officials – everyone, top to bottom – would spend fostering the relationships and making the connections they'd like to make is eaten up with teacher evaluations, legislation, standardized testing, and a million other pieces that just become cogs in the wheel of education, and cause school to become a place where kids and teachers can feel lonely and isolated.

The benefit of a fourteen-year window in this profession has shown me how times and access have changed, and these changes have frankly not all been for the better.

Teenagers today have less regard for the repercussions to their actions. They struggle to understand that something that they post on social media is there forever – they struggle to accept consequences and realize the long-term ramifications for making terrible choices.

This includes consequences for school violence.

4. Taking care of teachers, and supporting everyone's mental health

People have a tendency to forget that teachers are people, too. We have complex emotions and we process pain and trauma just like every other person in the world.

Teachers need to be free to express these feelings, to work through them, and to have resources available to them to assist when they are needed.

The stigma surrounding mental health is nothing but a detriment to the complex needs of all human beings, not just teachers.

There is a benefit of a fourteen-year window to see changes in society and in education, and also how the fears have changed – there is more to be concerned about now, even though the plans and systems that are in place to handle these situations are better.

These four topics, quite frankly, are just touching the surface. Ask a teacher or administrator who's been around for a while, and they may pick four completely different topics – and they would be critically important, too.

The purpose of this chapter – and every word of this entire book – is that we have to make it a priority to continue the conversation. There may be nothing more important in a successful society than how we educate and raise our children. It is that important, and it's equally important that we do all we can to support the people charged with educating them. Supporting these incredible professionals and caring for them at every level will help our society keep quality teachers in the profession – the shortage of teachers the United States is currently experiencing has been caused by more than just economics. If you ask a teacher why he or she left the profession, often money is not the reason. Instead, it's the disrespect and lack of regard for teachers as human beings that cause quality people to seek other careers. Often, the reason people leave is because schools are expected to fix societal failures at every level, and to do so with an incredible lack of resources and funding. Add to this the mental load that teachers carry, and it is often too much for some to bear, and so they leave. This is a tragedy that must be addressed before it is too late, and one way we can do that is to discuss and to support teachers in their mental health journeys.

Because after all, those teachers are people, too.

Chapter

Have A Little Faith And You'll See

Now that I have taught for fourteen years, it's interesting to look back on myself as that young, naïve, innocent-ish, teacher who was just starting her career. I don't even know that girl anymore, but I know that she was so happy to have a classroom of her own. I know that she was excited to work with teenagers, and I know that she poured her heart and soul into what she did with those kids every day. I also know that if I had it to do over again, there are so many things I would tell her, that I would warn her about. Then, maybe, some of the pain and the heartache would have been less, or maybe it wouldn't have happened at all.

The girl I was at 23 is a shadow to me now – I can barely see her. When I think really hard, I can conjure an image of her in my mind; I can imagine her walking into her classroom for the first time, staring out at the sea of empty desks, and I can remember the constant feeling of overwhelm that was pervasive for her throughout that school year.

And I can remember Kevin.

I remember him in snippets, in soundbites, and in waves. I remember the smiles we shared, but I also remember the troubled feeling he gave me in the pit of my stomach when he shared with me his fears about his future – and when other colleagues shared with me some of the strange interactions they had with him. I regret so much not listening to my gut. But the essence of our story is the not listening, and so instead, I choose to learn from it, and to go forward, doing a better job with all of my present and future students than I did with him.

Do I ever wish that I had handled it differently? Sure.

Have I ever wished I could go back and beg him not to do what he did? Absolutely.

There were so, so many things I wish I could have said to him. So much information I wish I would have had. Hindsight is fascinating in that way – it gives us more of the picture than the event as it is happening, which is simultaneously valuable and frustrating. If I could have had just even a small snippet of information more than what I had, maybe I could have talked him out of it. Logically, I know that isn't really true, but many, many nights I have laid awake thinking of what I would say to myself or to Kevin if given the chance.

*** *** ***

Years after we lost Kevin, I remember driving one evening down a country road with my windows down. As the wind blew into the car and onto my face, it whipped my hair around and dried some tears I didn't realize had even started – and as I tuned my focus in to the music that was playing on the radio, the song *Letter to Me* by Brad Paisley was playing.

If I could write a letter to me, I'd send it back in time to myself at 17 – and then I knew why I was crying. Regret is a powerful emotion, and it creeps up on us at times we may not even realize that it will matter. What would I have wanted Kevin to grow up and be able to say to himself 20, even 30 years down the road? What would I have said to him if I had just one more minute or one more day with him?

I know you're hurting, Kevin.

But I know, at seventeen, it's hard to see past Friday night.

Hang in there, Kevin. It will get better.

Have no fear; these are nowhere near the best years of your life.

It gets better – man, it gets so much better. You just have to hang in there. You just have to hold on.

Would that have made a difference? Would he have heard me? I don't know the answer to that, and at times the deafening sound of the silence I have kept all these years is coupled with such intense regret, even knowing that anything I said may not have made a difference at all. What would I, as an adult – close to 40 years old – say to myself? What exactly did I regret? Maybe it was not understanding who or what I was dealing with at the time. Maybe it was being a 23-year-old teacher who couldn't have processed those events and emotions even if I had tried right then. Maybe it was that I didn't pull back sooner and realize that something really wrong was happening. Even now, I'm not totally sure.

I wish you wouldn't worry, let it be.

I do wish I had asked him to hang on. I do wish I had

recognized the depth of his pain and had an idea of his illness – I know that isn't not my fault that I didn't. That realization took years, but I know it now, and I know it in my soul as an essential truth: it was not my fault.

I wish I had told him how much faith I really did have that he was capable of being a good person, that he could achieve all the success he wanted in his life, and that his fears were natural but that they would pass. I wish I had taken better care of his mentality during that time. I wish I would have said:

Have a little faith, and you'll see.

Knowing that I didn't say it or that I wasn't able to say it is something that I will regret for the rest of my life. It has shaped every part of my teaching career since April 20, 2007. I have dug deeper; I have loved harder; I have focused more on relationship-building. And I have done all of that in the name of what I should have done with Kevin.

It's interesting that at the time, this is what I thought I was, in fact, doing. It's interesting that at the time, I did what I was capable of, and that some people would say that what I did was enough, or that in some way it was above and beyond. But understanding that there was nothing I could have done that would have changed the outcome was a critical step in the healing process for me – no human is powerful enough to change what is meant to be.

Now, when I show up in a classroom full of kids every August, I think of Kevin, and I say a little prayer – not just for his eternal peace, but for the students who are entering my room, and for myself. I pray that I will give them what they deserve. I pray that my intense regrets about what happened with Kevin will not deter me from doing right by them. And I pray that I will let them see me for me.

I share my fears and anxieties and laughs and smiles with them because they need to know that teachers are people. I share my love for literature and writing with them because they need to know about passion. I share my daily "stuff" with them because they need to know that we are all in this together.

I have so many regrets about not saying these things to Kevin – and even more regret that it has taken me thirteen years to have the right words to say, period. But that is why this book exists. This book exists because, through regret and sadness, through heartache and tears, through fear and anger – I am doing it anyway. I am showing up anyway. I am teaching my classes anyway. I am being a mom and a wife and a human – anyway. And I've been doing it anyway since April 21, 2007.

I will never stop.

I will never stop fighting for myself, for my students, and for the humanity that must exist in education so that students, teachers and administrators alike can function in harmony with one another and meet the complex needs of everyone who steps into a school building on a daily basis.

And so, I tell this story here because this is not Kevin's story. It is mine. It is as real to me as any other moment in my life, and as impactful to me as anything that has ever occurred. It has given me the tools to be a better person and a better teacher, and though there is pain in this story – I think there is pain in every story, this part of the story is still mine.

The gift of this story expands far beyond how it has helped me to be a better teacher, because it has also helped me to be a better person. I think I'm a better mom and wife after learning what I have learned through and since we lost Kevin. But I have also learned that we didn't just lose Kevin – I have learned that the story of that loss is mine; I can hold it inside and keep it to myself forever, or I can share what it has taught me in the hope that someone, somewhere, will find some nugget of what I say to be useful. And if I help just one person through something hard by sharing my hard – well, then, that's a success.

Writing my story has been one of the most transformative experiences of my life. For so many years, I said nothing, I shared nothing, and I acknowledged nothing about the trauma that I experienced. To be silenced by that level of pain is unlike anything I have experienced since, and it has only in the last eleven months, as I have dug through the past to uncover this story yet again, that gaining the understanding of a level of pain like this and how to use it to work in the lives of others has happened for me.

I've had to remember that thinking of this on a much larger scale – the scale of helping other people – is the only way to tell this story successfully. It is the only way to truly move people and to connect with them in the ways that they crave to connect with others. Before I understood this, all I thought was that I could never share what I felt I truly knew in my heart about this incredibly sad and unusual story.

I have "turtle tendencies" as I have shared with all of you before, and it felt easier to just bury the experience and to not talk about it. But God shows us who we are over time, and as the time since Kevin's death has passed, God has used and grown me in immeasurable ways – and one of those ways is teaching me how to live in a way that is not driven by, or based on, fear.

One of the largest fears I've had to overcome is speaking the truth of this trauma aloud, sharing it with the world, knowing that there will be backlash because not everyone thinks of this story in the same way that I do – but doing it anyway. And doing it anyway has become one of the most important themes of my life – do it when you're scared; do it when you're unsure; do it when you don't feel ready. I've had to learn all of these lessons, mostly as an adult, and you know – I've cemented some hard truths through those lessons in the writing of this story. I've learned to accept that first year of teaching as a gift from the universe, one that I should, and will, use as my story going forward – a gift I will not be afraid to share with the world.

When the universe gifts you with something like this – and make no mistake: this story is a gift – be it a story or an experience that turns into a story, you must tell it. You must use the voice inside you to share who you are so that others can see you. To be here, in this moment, to tell this story is a gift so tremendous – one that I took for granted before as I shoved the pain and the experience out of my mind.

Only in the last five to seven years have I begun to really understand the ways that this story has connected me to other people, both those who knew Kevin and those who didn't. Human beings crave connections – and, after all, aren't stories the fibers that weave us all together in the end?

A Letter To The Younger Me

As I sit here and try to come up with the words to sum up what this 37-year-old version of me would say to the 23-year-old version of me, I feel that I should provide you, the reader, with some context. It is April 4, 2020 – Saturday. I am inside my home, where I have largely remained for the last 21 days – and will remain for the foreseeable future – as the world navigates a pandemic called COVID-19 and people whom we all know and love are dying.

This isn't exactly how I pictured writing this – in fact, if I had my druthers, I'd be at my favorite coffee shop, eating a lox bagel and sipping on a chai tea latte right now. Alas, that is not my currently reality. Instead, I'm in my makeshift home office, eating frosted donuts, sipping some basic breakfast tea, and praying my four-year-old doesn't wake up and demand my attention before I can crank out at least some of what is on my heart.

*** *** ***

Update: he's awake. I am writing with him on my lap asking rapid-fire questions. I think we are up to 46 questions asked and answered since he woke up ten minutes ago. Sigh.

*** *** ***

These are strange times we are living in, and yet the

solitude has provided some interesting opportunities for introspection that the noise of "regular" life never would seem to allow.

*** *** ****

So, if I may, I'd like to share with you some of the results of that solitude – a letter I have written to my 23-year-old self. Here is what I would say to her if I could meet her (and hug her) somewhere in space or time:

Dear Lindsey,

Hey there, you. How's that first year going? Not well? That's not surprising. I can't tell you a single person I know who loved their first year of teaching. Not one. I can't tell you a single person I know who didn't feel like they didn't have an earthly clue what they were doing during that first year. I can't tell you a single person I know who didn't think about quitting during that crazy first year. Is that you? Yeah? I thought so.

Well, I'm greeting you from the future, and hoping to impart some wisdom – maybe this will help, and maybe it won't – but hindsight is a funny part of life, and I hope this particular sharing of my own hindsight will at least bring you something of value.

This will be a year of your life that you experience unspeakable truth and tragedy. A year that will mold and shape you, challenge and scare you. This will be a year that, when you look back in a decade, you will realize shaped and grew you in ways that you could never imagine. This will be a turning point year, a year that shows you how to be both an adult and a professional. A year that leaves you so physically and emotionally exhausted that you won't be sure that you can go on.

But you will.

And going on is the theme of what I will share with you today.

In this year of your life, you will face challenges and fears unlike you have ever faced before, and none like you will ever face again. There will be moments that test the fibers of who you are, and there will also be moments that unravel the fibers of who you thought you were, only to weave them together over again, in a different pattern – because when you're done here this year, you're not going to be the same person you were when this whole adventure began.

But that's what I want to tell you about: the hardness, the difficulties you will face, and how you'll feel on the other side. And I need you to trust me – even though you think you're invincible and that you don't need anyone's help.

There will be moments this year that test you – there will be moments every year of your career that test you, that make you wonder if you went to school for the right thing, if you chose the right profession. There will be moments that make you wonder who you thought you were, and that will convince you that the answer to all of those questions is wrong. These moments will make you want to quit. To walk out of that classroom, and to never, ever go back.

But here's what you need to know: you will put more into your job – more energy, more passion, more heart – more everything than you ever thought possible. You will give to your students parts of yourself that you both don't think you ever had to give away, and that you don't think you have left to give. You will hug students on days that you yourself need a hug. You will wipe their tears on days that you yourself have cried. You will wipe tears from a student's cheeks when you think you have nothing left to give. You will stay after school or come in early and walk students through concepts or lessons that you're so tired you're not sure you can revisit – but you will.

And that, my sweet, young teacher, is the point.

When you think you can't keep going; when you think you have nothing left to give; when you have wiped your own tears and those of a student on the same day, that's when I need you to keep going. When you're ready to throw in the towel, I need you to hold on.

I need you to help them anyway. I need you to be there for them anyway. I need you to wipe their tears and listen to their rants and give them hugs anyway.

Because the beauty of what you do as a teacher will be in the things you do when you think you have nothing left. The beauty of what you do as a teacher will be where you can reach when you are positive your tank is empty and that it cannot be refilled. The beauty of what you do will occur when you reach to the depths of your heart and the depths of your soul and you grab onto something that you probably knew was there, but that you never thought you would need to access – and then you give it away.

This, my dear Lindsey, is when you will remember why you ever signed up to be a teacher in the first place. This – THIS – is when you will find out so much about your students. But the better part of these challenges is that during these moments, you will find out even more about yourself.

Before you can teach students to read and appreciate literature, you need to let them see you. Show them who you are as a human being: as a mother, as a daughter, as a wife, as a sister, as a friend. And if you do this – and you will – the ways that students will allow you to reach them will astound and inspire and impress you. It will move you in ways that you never thought you could be moved. And you will move them.

Beautiful things happen when human beings allow the connections we crave with other people to happen in a classroom – teenagers are incredible people. As you grow older and the age gap between you and your students widens, their passion and their raw emotion and their fearlessness will both scare and inspire you. You'll find yourself wishing to be more like them, and my challenge to you is that you would try to be more like them. Don't shy away from that rawness because you think you're too old, but instead grab ahold of it and look for ways you can apply their passion in your own life and in your own career.

Approach life with passion – leave your fears behind. Stop and savor the moments that have been gifted to you – even stories like Kevin's are a gift. You will be a better human and a better teacher because of what you learn from working with, and ultimately losing, Kevin. And I hope that doesn't make you timid. I hope that doesn't make you guarded. I hope that doesn't take away from the raw passion and the fearlessness with which you approach your role as an educator in these students' lives.

Instead, let it fuel you. Let it drive you forward, always making you better, always challenging you to be more passionate, more driven, better at what you do.

And whatever you do – always, always, put your relationships with them before the content you're teaching. The content will come, but not if they don't trust you. Not if they don't know the person you are and the stories that have woven that person together over the years. Please don't allow what has happened this first year to scare you, to cause you to shy away from your calling as a classroom teacher, to prevent you from reaching these young people the way they need and deserve to be reached.

Instead, let it drive you. Let it spur you forward, always with the back of your mind containing Kevin's story and how it shaped you. And speak his name. Speak it over and over and over again, allowing people to know that he has, in part, shaped the person who stands in front of them each and every day. You don't know this now, and someday you will – but Kevin has given you a piece of your identity as a human being and as a teacher. Kevin is irretrievably gone, but his legacy and his story, and what happened to you as a result are not.

So, please, sweet young teacher, use the gift that has been given to you.

And please – try not to be afraid. But when there comes a time that you are afraid – and that time will come – remember that the best, most productive, most selfless and humane thing you can do is to do it anyway. What is the "it" I am referring to?

"It" is everything. It is literally all of the things. Anything that scares you – do it anyway, and do not be driven by fear. Do not be driven by the tragedy that was Kevin's ending, for his was only one story – and though there are times when it feels like the only story, please do not let it be. Instead, embrace what is coming. Get to know these incredible young people. Let them know you.

And if you do this, you will have bounty and love and abundance in your life that I couldn't begin to express to you now. But trust me; the abundance is coming, and the beauty of it will take your breath away.

Your career is a gift. Please never stop knowing and believing that the voice God has given you in this world will reach some of the most incredible young humans the world has ever seen, and instead of just going through the motions, or instead of being driven by fear....

... do it anyway. You will be blessed abundantly when you do. I cannot wait to meet you on the other side of this, to look at you (most likely in a mirror) and to say, "Share your blessings with me—tell me about all of the gifts you've received in your life by sharing it with others."

And you will. Because you did.

And you – YOU – will be blessed.

With all my love and my wishes for abundance,

– Me

ACKNOWLEDGMENTS

On a chilly May evening in 2019, on a school night at a time that was far past my normal bedtime, my husband, Jon, tricked me into talking on the phone with a book publisher. I thought I was pitching one story to him, when in reality Jon hoped that I would be willing to crack open my heart and tell another one.

In a series of conversations over three or so months following that phone call, I allowed my heart to bleed the details of the story that shaped most of my adult identity, and *"Throwing Rocks"* was born. For playing the best trick that has ever been played, I would like to thank my husband for his unyielding, unrelenting, unconditional belief in the story that was in my heart and in its need to end up on paper. Thank you for that, and for always believing that I had a story to tell – and that I would somehow find a way to tell it.

Eventually, the book publisher from that late-night phone call became my friend. Tom Brew first met me for a breakfast date at Rosie's in Zionsville, Indiana that would ultimately change my trajectory forever. He and his company, Hilltop30 Publishing Group, gave life to the dream I've had since I was a little girl of being an author, of having my stories being told to more than just my friends and family.

Tom listened to the details of my story, and in my moments of doubt, sadness, and just plain fear – and there were many – held my hand and reminded me that stories are meant to be told, and even if one person benefits from the telling of Kevin's story, we have been successful. He reminded me that just because Kevin is in it, this story does not exclusively belong to Kevin, and that because I experienced Kevin's death, too, the story is also mine. Tom taught me, beyond what I already learned in therapy, to own my story, to be proud of it, and to tell it without reservation. Thank you, Tom, for believing not only in me, but in this story, and for giving it a place to come to life.

The dreams of little girls don't just appear. Little girls aren't born loving words and books and writing, and they are not born with songs like this one in their hearts. These songs and dreams must be cultivated over time, they must be fostered and encouraged, and given the courage to become reality. Mom, thank you. Thank you for wanting better for me than you had for yourself. Thank you for reading to me, for talking to me, for telling me what every mundane little object or moment meant so that all I heard, and all I can remember hearing, were words.

I fell in love with words because you first gave them to me. I fell in love with books because you first read them to me. I fell in love with literature and writing because you first taught me the stories of the world that are now and will forever be woven into the tapestry of my soul. Because of you, because of your dedication to a cause larger than yourself – to raising a future generation in a way that would make you proud and make the world better – I am who I am. Not only is this book a direct product of your stewardship and faith that I would find a different, better way, it is your voice. This is your life's work, mom, and I will never not know what you sacrificed to make sure that I had everything.

To my dad, who taught me to "find something I loved and find a way to get paid to do it," thank you. If it wasn't for your encouragement to stick to my passions, I might be an unhappy astronaut – let's face it, probably not; I'm terrible at Math – or I might be miserable in a cubicle somewhere wasting a perfectly good life doing something I hate. I sure do love what I am doing, and I am so glad I had the support from parents who understood my passions and cultivated that within me from day one. So, thank you for that phrase – while I may have listened a little too well, I'm thankful I listened at all.

Without these people, I could never – and would never – have been able to come to terms with what happened with Kevin. I wouldn't have been able to share that the story of what happened that first year of my career was a gift that was given to me by the universe. I would never have been able to view my transformation into the whole, healed person that I am today as anything other than a gift from the God of the Universe who loves and protects and cares for me. And so, I would like to thank Kevin. He did, after all, give me this story – albeit in a way that most people, myself included, would not want or expect.

Losing Kevin nearly caused me to quit teaching, to abandon my career, to allow myself to be ruled by the things that happened on that April night. Instead, I chose to thrive. I chose to tell his story – my story – in a way that acknowledges that all teachers and education professionals are impacted by traumas. I chose to share this in a way that highlights how I try, to this day, to continue to show up for and love on other people's babies as if they were my own, because that's what I believe is at the core of who we are as education professionals. But none of this would have been possible without Kevin. So, kiddo, thank you for scaring me, but thank you, also, for showing me my identity as a teacher and why that matters.

Kevin's story started with the most incredible mentorship – and the sage words of my kind, incredible mentor, who you read about here in Kevin's story, stick with me today. My mentor taught me to smile in the face of adversity, to always treat people with the utmost respect as humans and as professionals, and to never take for granted the gift of my ability to communicate about literature and writing with teenagers. He taught me that teachers are often so much more than teachers – to students, to themselves, to communities, all of it. And he showed me what it really meant to truly be someone's mentor. My friendship with my mentor spanned over a decade and we shared many seasons of our lives together. This past July, I lost him to pancreatic cancer, though I lost pieces of him before that – and this year, when school started and the absence of his physical body from this earth I could feel in my bones, and I said my annual prayer for Kevin's eternal peace, I added my mentor to this prayer. I have unimaginable gratitude for his guidance, for his friendship, and for his love. I miss him every day of my life, and the ache for his absence will be eternal, as will the understanding of the gift of his presence.

The healing of my heart began the summer after Kevin's accident, and the beauty of that healing brought me the best friend I never had, and always longed for, when I was a lonely teenager – aren't all teenagers lonely in different ways? She was Kevin's counselor, and she felt his death as deeply, if not more so, than I did. Losing Kevin gave me the gift of her, and like my mentor, we walked through many seasons of this life together – happy ones, sad ones, funny ones, and ridiculously unbelievable ones. Through all of these seasons, she's held me up, she's championed me, she's allowed me to champion her, and she has loved me at my least lovable. Thank you, KJ, for being my BFF and for always, always, holding me when I ugly cry.

Oh, Trish. There are not enough pages in the world to thank you the way you deserve to be thanked. This book is for you – and I know that, wherever you are, you know that I healed my heart enough to be strong enough to tell this story. That heart healing began with you, and on the day that I knew this book would come to life, I looked at my husband and said, "Man, I wish Trish were here so I could tell her about this." He smiled at me and said, "She knows." And I knew then that he was right.

Thank you for allowing me to bring my broken heart to you, and thank you for showing me how to put it back together. Thank you for the magic that was your soul, and for sharing it with me. Thank you for making me eat that cheeseburger and throw those rocks. Without your home-work assignments, I cannot tell you the path my life would have taken. I can only share that I fear it would not be this one. Rest peacefully, my dear friend. And know that some-where, someone found their voice because of you.

To every student I have ever taught, and to the ones I will teach in the future: thank you. Thank you for letting me see you, and for allowing me to be seen. Thank you for your humanity, your boldness, your unfiltered passion – without this influence in my life, my own flame would have been extinguished long ago. It is for you, too, that I tell my story. But more than anything, each of you are why I need this world to take care of its teachers – you and everyone who will come after you deserve teachers who are healed and whole and imperfect who can walk through this phase of life with you and help you to come out better – not just as students, but as people.

To my boys, Jack and Andrew, for reminding me that almost nothing is truly about me. Thank you for watching every move I make and for learning the type of men and people you will become by watching your dad and me. Without this profound knowledge, I would never have had the courage to pursue this dream.

Neither of you are old enough now to read this story, but one day you will be. When you are, I will share that I wrote it for you. I wrote it so you would know and under-stand me a little better, but also so you would know that

I will be forever grateful that my therapist Trish gave me the homework assignment that saved my life.

stories – including the parts of each of yours that are yet to unfold – are meant to grow us, to shape us, and to make us better, not scare us away from participating in the world. To my two greatest gifts: I love you. I want nothing for each of you but beautiful, magical lives, but I also know, and I hope I can impart to you, that sometimes beauty and magic arise from the ashes of a former life or events caused by pain. That beauty is OK and worthy, too, and I hope that each of you has the courage to share those lessons and how they shaped you when the time comes, both with the people in your lives and with any future children you each may have.

Thank you both for the gifts you bring to my life. I would not be capable of anything without you; I would not be complete without you. Your hearts and your spirits are my greatest treasures.

The Acton family.

WHAT THEY'RE SAYING

There is an unspoken bond that tethers teachers to our students. We know this about our calling, and we secretly believe that this connection is sacred and real and true.

But sometimes this connection exposes us to lessons far beyond the classroom walls. *Throwing Rocks* presents a hauntingly unique and tragically universal teaching experience. In the hallowed space of story-telling, Lindsey reveals layers of expectation and shame, and invites us into the inner trauma, heartache, vulnerability and love of every teacher in every classroom.

Though her experience is unique, this love is universal. *Throwing Rocks* is a story of duality, how a person can be both exactly who they are – and nothing like themselves – in the exact same instant.

– Carrie Rosebrock
Professional Learning Specialist,
Central Indiana Educational Services Center

*** *** ***

In *Throwing Rocks*, author Lindsey Acton opens a window to her soul to share a story that, unfortunately, is all too common for educators. As she describes her struggles as a beginning teacher, she establishes awareness for an all too often ignored need for educators.

It is a compelling story that leads us to a better understanding of the challenges teachers face beyond the classroom. We must recognize the need for us to take care of our own mental health and access to the services to do so. Considering the struggles that educators all face every day, the amazing thing is not how many people leave the profession, but how many choose to stay.

– Dr. David A. Wintin, Principal
Hauser Junior-Senior High School, Howe, Indiana

*** *** ***

Trauma and Post Traumatic Stress Syndrome have long been associated with our soldiers who have fought in wars. Only recently have we as a society begun to recognize such issues in our children.

Slowly, schools have begun to screen children for social-emotional issues such as trauma, depression, and anxiety to develop partnerships with mental health services, and to initiate programs of social-emotional learning to help students. But as Lindsey Acton, in her book *Throwing Rocks*, clearly demonstrates to us, "What about Teachers?" What services are there for teachers who are on the front lines of education?

Throwing Rocks provides us a compellingly true story of a young teacher who is faced head-on with real life trauma loss, death, and fear. It is a must-read for every educator, as well as for parents. Lindsey makes us aware of the compassion teachers have for their students, the dedication to education, but most importantly the realities and struggles that can last a lifetime. Once you start reading, I guarantee you will not be able to put it down!

– Dr. Terry McDaniel
Program Coordinator, K-12 Administration, Ph.D, Ed.S,
Indiana State University

*** *** ***

In *Throwing Rocks*, author Lindsey Acton delicately and carefully weaves together a story, combining her personal life and that of a troubled teenager she thought might end hers. Acton writes a book on how she worked through emotional trauma stemmed from what she thought would be a horrific incident, and does so in a way that brings together vulnerability, heartbreak, and hope for her future.

For anyone who has suffered through emotional trauma, Acton offers emotional insight into her life, and how schools can provide support for their education community. But more importantly, she illustrates the importance of releasing what's inside, letting go, and moving forward.

– Kym Klass, author,
One More Day: A powerful true story of
suicide, loss, and a woman's newfound faith